SHARING THE WORLD

Other Luce Irigaray titles available from Continuum:

SHARING THE WORLD

Luce Irigaray

continuum

Continuum

Continuum International Publishing Group
The Tower Building   80 Maiden Lane
11 York Road   Suite 704
London SE1 7NX   New York NY 10038
www.continuumbooks.com

© Luce Irigaray 2008

British Library Cataloguing-in-Publication Data
A catalogue record for this book is available from the British Library.

ISBN–10: HB: 1–8470–6034–X
ISBN–13: HB: 978–1—8470–6034–1

Library of Congress Cataloging-in-Publication Data

Irigaray, Luce.
  Sharing the world / Luce Irigaray.
    p. cm.
  ISBN 978-1-84706-034-1
  1. Other (Philosophy) 2. Transcendence (Philosophy) I. Title.
  B2430.I74S53 2008
  194--dc22
                              2007037031

Typeset by Fakenham Photosetting Limited, Fakenham, Norfolk
Printed and bound in Great Britain by MPG Books Ltd, Bodmin, Cornwall

Contents

Acknowledgements

During a whole winter, I translated *Sharing the World* from the French. I devoted two or three hours each day to this work, which I consider both stimulating and fruitful. At the beginning of the spring, the translation was finished; at least I believed that. I could not imagine how many things would be added, removed, modified with respect to my original version. The first changes have been made or suggested by Andrea Wheeler and Laine Harrington, who typed the manuscript. Then, I submitted the typed text to Mary Green and, for weeks, it circulated between us with an intense work from both. The comments of a philosopher were still lacking. Stephen Pluháček – who is a philosopher, knows my work and has already translated, alone or with Heidi Bostic, two of my books – was fortunately on sabbatical leave. In a truly friendly way, he accepted to be the guarantor for the final version delivered to the publisher.

I heartily thank each of them for their callaboration in this English version of *Sharing the World*. I am particularly grateful to Stephen Pluháček for sharing with me a part of his sabbatical, a time that he needed to repose and write a book of his own. I hope that Stephen, Mary, Laine and Andrea will receive, for their own lives, the benefit of this generous help.

Introduction: The Transcendence of the Other

When the world corresponds to the transcendence projected by a single subject as the horizon of the totality of all that exists, this world converts time into space. Although such a transcendence represents a temporal project on the part of the subject, the fact that this subject ensures, from a unique standpoint, the gathering or the closure of the whole of finite things results in the world closing up, even in advance, in a circle. The intuition of the infinite can remain, but the dynamic, indeed the dialectical, relations between time and space somehow or other freeze. Passing from one horizon to another, from one epoch of history to another, will thus not happen without some harm: for example, without war according to Hegel, without destruction or deconstruction according to Heidegger.

In contrast, if the transcendental also has its origin in a respect for the irreducible difference of the other really considered as other, in the fact that their otherness is thus never knowable nor appropriable by myself – although it appears limited to my perceptions and even my intuitions – then transcendence no longer amounts to merely making objective a projection of my own subjectivity. So long as the other subject remains alive and free with respect to another world, especially to my world, time and space are kept in a dialectical process between us in an always indefinite and open way.

It is true that I then have to renounce projecting in a solitary manner – or in a manner shared by all the subjects of one epoch who are presumed to be the same – the horizon of a world as a transcendence. As soon as I recognize the otherness of the other as irreducible to me or to my own, the world itself becomes irreducible to a single world: there are always at least two worlds. The totality that I project is, at any moment, questioned by that of the other. The transcendence that the world represents is thus no longer one, nor unique. And if the gesture of projecting the totality of a world can remain a gesture that has something to do with transcendence, to recognize the partial nature of such a transcendence is even more transcendental. It reopens the autological circle of the transcendental horizon of a single subject in the name of this truth: the human real is formed by two subjects, each one irreducible to the other. As each has his or her own way of projecting a horizon that gathers the totality of existing beings, the transcendental gesture that is fitting to their human existence becomes one of building with the other a relation in which space and time are, at any moment, in-finite and in becoming.

Man transcends himself towards a world in order to give himself a unity through a projection of all that he perceives towards a present, but always future, horizon. Man needs such a transcendental project to acquire an identity of his own with regard to his origin, especially his maternal origin. However, through this gesture he not only projects what he is, but also a perception of all the beings in the midst of which he finds himself. The unity that he forms or delimits in this way is thus not only his, but also that of an emergence which he imagines he represents with respect to his surroundings.

In reality, what the masculine subject constitutes is a sort of new placenta in which to be sheltered in separating off from his natural birth. This projection of a horizon is necessary for him to distance himself from an adherence to, or confusion with, his maternal or uterine origin. And the historical epoch that he elaborates in this way is only a new modality or figure of his attempt to acquire an identity of his own with respect to this origin. This construction is problematic for two reasons from a transcendental or ideal standpoint relative to human reality. No doubt, it signifies an intention to surpass an individualization already partially gained, a status already acquired, yet it is not certain that this corresponds to a specifically human reality. It indicates rather a stage towards the advent of this human reality.

Projecting a world does not necessarily amount to attaining a human world. Furthermore, such a projection exists starting from the intention of man alone. It is thus both partial and biased. And when the world is given back to us as human reality, it imposes upon us all a conception of this reality which is far from expressing or unveiling its totality, and thus its truth. Such a failure is all the more serious since the horizon of the world, which in this way determines meaning, appears in terms of requirements, a prioris, laws, ideals, which paralyse the becoming of a different human reality, notably by preventing it from transcending itself towards a world appropriate to it. Furthermore, because this projection of a world comes before any representation, judgement, indeed any conscious feeling, it cannot be questioned in a rational way. It is even prior to any word, and a fortiori prior to any possible dialogue. Any verbal exchange is presumed to ensure its permanence through statements that are, in reality, tautological with regard to the foundation of the world. In this enveloping horizon, which is at every moment finite, the debate of man with himself and those who are the same as him amounts in some way to a worn-out repetition of an already given reality and truth. This debate is without any freedom until a subject or an event of the milieu – an explosive saturation, for example – tears the horizon and compels man to project another, which does not happen without some disaster or rejection. The collapse of transcendences or ideals does not take place without causing harm – to man, to those who are the same as him, to his world and environment. And the proposal of new values is generally contested until the milieu becomes imbued with them and imposes them as an almost eternal reality or truth, after it has become immune to their novelty.

In fact, such a conception of the world and of human reality leaves only an illusory freedom to man himself, and a spontaneity without any further possible transcendental realization. At least this is the case for most people, which can be appraised by the use they make of a surplus of energy – for example, of sexual energy. An energy that could be unfurled as the horizon of a world built with a view towards a sharing of desire with the other is instead expended in secondary, animalistic, solitary, 'shameful' or warring activities … There where one ought to appeal to freedom in order to accomplish human reality as such, it no longer exists because it is harnessed by ideals or obligations that do not take into account the most demanding human imperative: to cultivate the development of an energy, that is always and already bound to the other, towards the elaboration of a specifically human transcendence.

Freedom, in a way spontaneous and autonomous with respect to the historical foundation of the world, is able, at any moment, to be converted into transcendence without cutting itself off from the source of its impetus. Instead of projecting itself onto the horizon of a world, it must be safeguarded, reserved, brought to a standstill or hemmed in before the other as other, an other who is recognized in his, or her, transcendence, and with whom the matter will be one of elaborating a relation without abolishing either the duality of the subjects or the difference(s) between them.

To say that human reality is determined by the whole of what exists exclusively as beings in the world probably obeys the necessities and limits of masculine subjectivity. The self of man is first received from an other who, surrounding him, remains imperceptible as other: his mother. Because of his lack of recognition of the mother as a transcendence in whom he first has his origins, man projects the origin of his self onto the totality of the world, unless he extrapolates it from God. The other who is close to him, the other from whom he receives himself, is not recognized as transcendence. The mother, and later the woman, remain confused with a world that is solely natural, from which it is necessary to emerge in order to become a man; they are not recognized with a full humanity that transcends itself in a way different from that of a man. The mother, a woman, exist starting from an en-stasis and not an ec-stasis with regard to themselves. Their world is constituted through respecting the other within oneself, and not by projecting the totality of what exists outside oneself, as man does.

The expression of transcendence requires different modalities on the part of man and of woman. For woman, what matters is to withdraw or to limit herself in order to open within her self a place of hospitality for the other, without appropriation, fusion or confusion. For man, the question is instead one of acquiring an identity of his own with respect to the first dwelling or environment from which he has received himself, by projecting, into an always future present, the ex-sistence of a possible world of his own. This manner of differing from her does not take into consideration the mother as other, except in a negative way. It represents an attempt to go away without any return. To impose a world of his own is, on the part of man, often an unconscious way of replying to a first dwelling in the mother, to a desire to remain in woman, to a necessity of begetting children within her. Man tries to envelop, by his world, by his transcendence, the one by whom he has been enveloped, nourished. Which most of the time deprives her of a transcendence of her own.

Between him and her and, in return, between her and him, the existence – ex-sisting – of the reality of a difference, including in the way of forming a world and expressing a transcendence of one's own, is lacking. The possibilities of the one and the other then become paralysed or unrecognized. And this deprives humanity of the most fertile source of its impetus, of its freedom, a source from which the outpourings are constant if each one remains faithful to one's own world. At each moment, a different way of relating to the transcendental frees up an energy that might be fixed and frozen in the horizon of a unique totality. Thus, for each one and for the two, the impetus and the limit, which ensures the return to the source of the self, are safeguarded. Thanks to the respect for the transcendence of the other as irreducible to one's own, each discovers, at each moment, a new impetus toward the in-finite – or infinite – through the recognition of the finiteness of one's own world. The in-finite can again become the horizon of the intention of each one thanks to accepting that the totality of the world that is one's own is, for its part, necessarily finite.

This impetus toward the in-finite – or infinite – is then able to promote or produce as in-finite – or infinite – the becoming of the relation between the two worlds, at least so long as these worlds are considered in their duality and each subjectivity cares about constituting one's own world with the intention of transcending the human reality in which he or she is already situated. In this reality, the other and its transcendental project are already present. Each subject is always already affected by the existence of the other: each one, always and already, is in relation to and with the other. This is the case at a natural level, through the intuition and experience of belonging to the same species, and it is also the case at a transcendental level, through the fact that they ex-sist in the world. But this transcendental is perverted in its intentionality if it does not take into consideration the duality of worlds. This presupposes that each subject questions him- or herself about their intentional relation regarding the other before projecting a unique and anticipatory horizon onto the totality of all that exists. Questioning myself about my relation to the other as such offers the possibility of turning that through which I am always and already affected by this other into transcendence. The real coexistence that formed our being together can thus become a coexistence of intentionalities of which the transcendental dimension will be more in accordance with human reality or truth. The transcendental project will then become raised more to the level of a conscious and freely decided intention towards non-human existence, the self, and the other recognized in his or her difference, both natural and transcendental.

In fact, going no further than those who are similar to oneself leads to transcendence itself getting bogged down either in a natural belonging or in belonging to a supposedly common world. The relation to non-human existing, but even more to human existing, has to be rethought in the horizon of a reality in which being in relation with the other cannot be overshadowed by projecting a world of one's own. This projecting remains possible only as long as the relations take place between those who are alike, those who are presumed to share a unique and common view of the world. The error of Western philosophy in part lies there: having intended to carry on with human individuation starting from a single transcendence corresponding to the necessities of the masculine subject. In such a unique design towards the whole of existing beings, woman cannot discover her transcendental possibilities. And, because of a failure to recognize a double human subjectivity, a part of his own possibilities remains veiled to man himself.

No doubt, the nature of the double – or rather triple – transcendence that in this way becomes outlined, discovered as possible and even necessary, remains partly veiled. It is only indirectly that such a possibility, and even necessity, proves to be a means of letting blossom the being-in-the-world of the feminine subject, as well as the human relation between subjects who are naturally different. For this advent, the task of the feminine subject is crucial. Woman has to separate off from the world that is imposed on her as unique, found a world of her own and also the means of coexisting with a world irreducible to her own. Because the world that takes form in this way represents progress in human becoming only on the condition that it does not impose itself as a unique world blindly laying down the law on all that exists. It is important that the feminine world take into account in its foundation and its legitimation the transcendence of the other, thus allowing each human reality to exist – and ex-sist – in the midst of existing beings as a whole.

Woman is led to recognize the transcendence of the other because this gesture is part of the foundation and development of her own transcendence. But it is necessary that she discover herself, and by herself, what can ensure a transcendental basis to her world. It is not a masculine being, even a divine one, that could alone provide woman with a transcendental status. Even in this case, she still remains dwelling in and subjected to the world of the other. She does not found a world in accordance with her necessities and possibilities, which requires a transcendental ground of her own, in addition to that of man, recognized as a human reality destined to be in relation to and with the other.

To stress the relation to the other as an irreducible dimension of human reality and freedom shifts the concern regarding temporality. It is no longer a matter of persisting or subsisting, but of keeping alive the becoming of oneself, of the other, of the relations between the two.

What is at stake in the becoming as becoming is probably specifically human. But, instead of remaining a necessary task in our present existence – and ex-sisting – it has been put off into the beyond. Becoming would be dependent on our achieving another world, another nature, and not on our transforming this world and our own nature. The necessity of projecting the achievement of our human being into another world, making it dependent on a transcendence extraneous to humanity itself, could be explained by the formation of a world where the transcendence of the other as other is unrecognized. In such a case, a part of human reality – and, therefore, human reality in its totality – is deprived of its inherent motivations and the reasons in which they find their source and their impetus. This could result in one subject representing Being for the other, but this does not yet amount to reaching Being for oneself by freely assuming a transcendence able to found a world of one's own. The affective dimension of such a world ceaselessly projects itself towards its surpassing so that it can remain an affect of one's own while becoming a shared relation thanks to the mediation of a transcendence respectful of the duality of freedoms and truths. This implies that one cares about maintaining an impetus but also a limitation on each side, having in mind a becoming that is sustained, both as a world of one's own and as a relation to the other, through the relation between the two worlds.

The limit of freedom can take place in various ways, and freedom itself can receive its impetus from a more or less human real and reality. In the unfolding of Western thought, freedom has not yet been rooted in accordance with the specifically human task that consists of passing from nature to culture in the relation between human subjectivities. If this blossoming of a possible – and, moreover, necessary – becoming has not yet happened, this could be explained by the fact that the difference between man and woman has not been considered as allowing, indeed needing, a transcendental ground. Providing this difference with such a horizon requires that the impetus of freedom originate in a specifically human real and reality and not in sexual or procreative instincts, which are not strictly human. This presupposes that the spontaneous energy which attracts the sexes to one another will be converted into affects, into feelings, into thoughts, without for all that renouncing or annihilating such an energy. To cultivate sexual attraction as an original impetus in the relations between humans is a task that Western culture has not cared about with the seriousness that it deserves. Nevertheless, it is through this task that humanity can distance itself from other species, discovering an impetus and limits of its own. Which makes the construction of a truly human world possible.

Human freedom is neither mere natural spontaneity nor mere impetus arising from a retroactive effect of the anticipation of the totality of a world by a unique subject. Human freedom is more mysterious in its origin and its finality. It resembles the sap that comes out of a delicate plant, and that grows or withers depending on whether or not the surroundings in which it appears are favourably disposed towards its existence, its becoming. The welcome its impetus receives from the other and the contribution that the other, in turn, makes to its impetus also act upon the possibilities of it being based with more knowledge and more respect for human and non-human reality, for truth. Consequently, the projection of a world of one's own and that of a shared world become more faithful to what exists and, if this projecting means a transcendental gesture with respect to existence, the aim is now to cultivate this existence in accordance with its own life rather than towards its mastery.

Founded upon the respect for non-human existence, for oneself, and for the other considered in his or her difference, freedom loses the unfathomable nature that a subject existing only in a solitary way can feel with regard to it, even if it is limited. Freedom is constrained, at each moment, to re-define or adjust itself according to the human or non-human beings which surround it. This does not mean that freedom must renounce its impetus but that it must discover an economy compatible with the impetus of the other, in his or her life and transcendental intention. Freedom must, at every moment, limit its expansion in order to respect other existing beings and, even more, to find ways of forming with them a world always in becoming where it is possible for each human or non-human living being to exist – or ex-sist.

In such a world, the freedom of each living being, and of human being in particular, does not project itself, from a unique ground, towards the horizon of the totality of existing beings. Its impetus and its limits – a term which is more suitable than deprivation, in my opinion – enter, at each moment, into a dialectical process in which the other participates by what they bring but also by what they remove as possibilities of life, both natural and transcendental. Such a process takes part in the constitution of a world of one's own according to the possibilities of each one. It is also at work in structuring a relational world between each existing being and each other. This aspect is especially critical between humans whose reality, both natural and transcendental, is different: woman and man.

If freedom, in this way, reveals itself to be more free than it could have been, it also meets with a limit that it must continuously confront because of the irreducible duality of the human real and reality. Not taking into account the existence – or possible ex-sisting – of the other, in fact amounts to depriving oneself of some freedom both by reducing the original impetus and by only partially founding that which determines the transcendental impetus. This makes human freedom as such impossible. Because this freedom cannot exist – or ex-sist – without taking into account the irreducible duality of humanity, and the fact that the relations between two human existences cannot remain at or return to the level of a mere natural impetus.

The Path Towards the Other

The Opening of a Threshold

The path towards the other is first a path towards the infinite, an infinite in which both I and the other risk losing ourselves. A threshold is lacking that marks the limits of the world of each one. Also lacking is the difference between us, which allows the opening of a threshold. In fact, a threshold must exist for each one, but it must as well exist between the one and the other. Each one has, or ought to have, limits which set borders between one's self and the beyond. This self comprises all that belongs to a world of one's own: the way in which the subject relates to itself, to the other, to the world, but also to the cultural environment in which this subject lives, an environment which takes part in our subjectivity and is too often confused with identity itself. To recognize the existence of another subjectivity implies recognizing that it belongs to, and constitutes, a world of its own, which cannot be substituted for mine; that the subjectivity of the other is irreducible to my subjectivity.

To assert that a single sort of subjectivity exists for humanity amounts to being unaware of the parameters that define this subjectivity, especially in its relational dimensions. In any case, it is too soon to affirm this, because we do not yet know all the possible ways or modes through which a subject can constitute itself and its world. Such an affirmation would mean imposing our manner of being, and Being, on other cultures.

Nevertheless, one difference at once appears as universal: sexual, or better sexuate, difference. Of course, it is worked out in various ways by different cultures but it maintains constant dimensions with regard to the connection between nature and culture, especially concerning that which already exists and that which is still to be constructed of the relations of one's own body to the self and to the other.

It thus seems right to start, or start again, from this determination of subjectivity in order to define the limits corresponding to one's own world and the way of laying out or inhabiting a threshold. When such indications are supported by the connection between natural givens and their most elementary cultural elaboration, they do not represent compulsory norms imposed by a culture on others according to its own necessities. They permit deconstructing the artifice of a tradition while also elaborating potential universal ways of being in relation with oneself and with the other.

Appropriation has dominated the rules of construction in a monosubjective culture. Recognizing one's own limits, as well as the existence of the other as irreducible to one's own existence, and searching for the means of entering into relations with him, or her, will then substitute for appropriation. Such necessities or cultural obligations can appear as universal duties insofar as they are based on a universal given: the division of humanity into two sexes who really live in different worlds. Certainly it is no longer a matter of coexisting in a world built by only one part of humanity with its own survival in mind. Rather the question is about the world that each one has to build in order to dwell in their own subjectivity and in this way be able to meet with the subjectivity of the other and enter into exchange with respect for differences, that is, for what is proper to each one.

The parameters that are to be treated by each one in order to carry out such a task are not the same. To cultivate the relations with the one who brought you into the world does not involve the same elements for those who are the same as her or different from her – that is, for a female or a male subject. And to have recourse to the abstraction of a paternal law for remedying a supposedly amorphous empathy in the first relations with the mother cannot solve the passage from nature to culture: rather, it evades the problem by repressing it. The same, the intervention of the precious paternal seed cannot be the sole leaven for a cultivation of the original link with the one who brings us into the world. The task is other and still to be accomplished, by woman as well as by man.

Whether desire tends towards the other and fulfils itself outside oneself or preserves in the self a welcome for the other also represents a different relational space for man and for woman. Received as a given that accompanies one's own body, this requires a cultivation of the relations to the self and to the other that is not the same. To give birth in oneself or outside oneself as well means an irreducible dimension of belonging to a sex.

3

Laying down a masculine law – at a linguistic, civil or religious level – on a nature that is supposedly undifferentiated, be it the mother or the child, does not correspond to a cultivation of differences. Such a gesture does not sufficiently take into account the respective subjective positions, simply opposing nature and culture when it is really a question of nature and culture on both sides. Patterns operating almost as a prioris have prevented man and woman from elaborating what begetting and loving mean with respect to oneself, to one's own body, but also to the relational context in which it is situated. Having become an imperative imposed from the outside in which, what is more, the need of an instinctive satisfaction remains, giving birth has not contributed to the subjective becoming of man and woman – the child thus being in more than one account the death of the parents, as Hegel wrote.

Without working out the relational context in which it arises, desire remains or falls back into instinct, an instinct the connotations of which sometimes seem more uneducated than in the animal world itself. The attraction for the other loses any moderation. It remains a mere vital impulse, unless it is determined by cultural components that have nothing to do with entering into relations with another subject: possession, subjection, appropriation. Without being aware of one's own world and recognizing the world to which the other belongs, entering into relations with him, or her, proves to be impossible. This additional clarity about what or who a human being is must be rethought, reformulated, and thus along with it a great part of the content of our discourses and behaviours. This discovery already opens a threshold with regard to a previous culture, and perceiving this threshold could help to sense the threshold or thresholds that exist between myself and the other, the other and myself.

Thus silence will no longer be that which has not yet come to language, that which is still lacking words or a sort of ineffability that does not merit interest from language. Silence is the speaking of the threshold. If this silence does not remain present and active, the whole of discourse loses its most important function: communicating and not merely transmitting information. Then dialogue becomes impossible. In no dialogue can everything be said, and it is recognizing the necessity of something unspeakable and its preservation that allows an exchange of words between two different subjects. It is thanks to silence that the other as other can exist or be, and the two be maintained. Relations between two different subjectivities cannot be set up starting from a shared common meaning, but rather from a silence, which each one agrees to respect in order to let the other be. Entering into communication requires the limits, always effective, of a unique discourse, access to a silence thanks to which another world can manifest itself and take place.

To claim that nothing would be there where the word is lacking (cf. the argument of Heidegger, notably in the text 'The Way to Language' in *On the Way to Language*, translated by Peter D. Hertz, Harper, San Francisco and New York, 1982, pp.109–136), means to deny the existence of the other and of that which remains unspeakable where two worlds join together. Western philosophy has cared about the relations of the subject to things, and about the relations between things and the world, but very seldom about the relations between two subjects, especially two different subjects – the only place where speaking is really indispensable, but a speaking that only happens from a lack of word(s). Which does not necessarily give rise to sadness or frustration, but rather to the joy of opening to an other, source of a new saying. Certainly, we then renounce mastering the whole and the power of all by ourselves giving names to things, and, in this way, arranging them in a single world. But this assenting to one's own limits corresponds to reaching out to the other as other, to receptiveness to a different language, to the discovery of a still-unknown world in which work and mastery do not simply impose their law on us. Nor listening to that which is always and already determined by a single statement in speaking.

Each subjectivity henceforth has before it a source of words foreign to that in which it dwells – thus not a space opened by a language that is already shared, but a horizon which opens beyond its limits.

Even if there are intersections between the saying of the other and one's own, this does not prevent the sites from which words arise from being different for each one. Listening is thus never simple, and it is not from a single saying that the meaning offered to the other for sharing could be received. It is necessary to listen to the saying of the other, and to discover a saying that could be fitting for the two. This saying cannot be already said or foreseen by a previous discourse: it arises from a mutual listening, from the sense that is discovered thanks to the confidence of two subjects in one another, from the search for words that correspond to this reciprocal abandon.

Patience is imperative: the future is not defined here by the past, and the house, notably of language, is not yet built. Sometimes, we hardly reach the threshold, starting from which it happens that we call to the other, that we invite him, or her, to share our home, without yet leaving a well-known place in order to approach a region that is unfamiliar to us.

And yet, nearness to the other cannot amount to sharing a territory, to a spatial closeness. The other as other remains remote from us, whatever the neighbourhood in which we are situated. And insofar as we recognize that we are remote from one another, we can begin to come near. This approach cannot be merely spatial, at least in the sense of a physical closeness. But nor can it stop with a complicity in the same culture: the same background of ideas, of opinions. On the contrary, this risks veiling the otherness of the other through the sharing of a common third, which gives us the illusion of being close. It is essential to be aware of co-belonging to a spatial or cultural environment and to deconstruct it so that each can discover whether and how this environment is or is not appropriate to oneself.

Before wanting to approach the other, it is advisable to wonder about oneself and one's own manner of dwelling. It is important to have a view of one's own faithfulness to that which is proper to one. And often it will be necessary to turn back on our path in order to question ourselves about where we are already situated. If we are not dwelling where we ought to dwell, being what or who we are, we are not prepared for an encounter with the other. We are only able to impose on the other our alienation, misunderstanding, or ignorance. Opening a threshold in order to approach the other requires that we dwell where we can and should be.

Without overrunning our limits. Only these allow us to have access to the other by respecting ourselves. If we are not faithful to ourselves, approaching the other proves to be impossible. What we could then experience would only be appropriation, leading us astray from what is proper to us and proper to the other. What is proper to each world as well. Confusing a part of the other with ourselves makes us lose an accurate perception of the place where we dwell. Henceforth no environment maintains a real distance between living beings and things. And the background against which they dwell and relate to one another becomes an illusory construction which leads them to their ruin.

Nearness to the other, or better with the other, appears in the possibility of elaborating a common world with him, or her, a world which will not destroy the world proper to each one. This common world is always in becoming. A living being, especially a human living being, is irreducible to a thing. It cannot exist once and for all, neither in itself nor towards the other or the world. If we consider humans as things, their becoming amounts to a decline, and that through which they were truly human disappears: a becoming that is partly decided and ruled by oneself. A becoming that, of course, is also modified by the other. But instead of speaking of paths that cross each other ad infinitum, of cuts in the one or the other resulting from an unfolding of spatial proximity, of furrows which open up, it would be better to speak of building openings that are deliberately arranged for having access to the other – thus of thresholds.

On the borders of our own dwelling, thresholds will prepare a meeting with the other: thresholds on the horizon of a world allowing us to leave it and to welcome the other, thresholds also on the border of oneself, if it is possible to distinguish between the two. To build such openings requires from us an active undertaking but also a letting be: an economy that is too little known in our Western culture, and one that meeting with the other as other constrains us to discover, to cultivate. It will no longer be only a matter of existing or Being, of trying to let the other and things be, but also of uniting, at each moment, our quest for existing or Being to that of letting us be. Making this way towards letting be will take place in our relations with nature and with the other. Trusting in the contribution that the otherness of the other will provide us with, agreeing to receive until we become changed, without for all that renouncing ourselves – that is what a threshold must give us access to. Opening a welcome through working out an appropriateness to ourselves, through a gathering within ourselves.

To Venture Upon the Path

If in ourselves, in our dwelling, space and spacing must be safeguarded and cultivated, the arrival at the borders of ourselves, of our world, opens out onto new places – places that are still virgin or to be cleared. We can venture into them alone and try to appropriate them, to make them our own. But if the threshold has been built with the intention of meeting with the other, there is no doubt that, beyond this threshold, his or her call will join our own, paving new paths in the spaces opened.

Once the threshold has been built, if we agree to cross it, we then have to discover the path, or the paths, that lead towards the other. In such an undertaking, we must listen to the attraction that has encouraged us to leave our own dwelling. Does it remain once the threshold has been passed? Where does it lead us? Do we hear a call from the other that corresponds to the call we have already heard? Could it guide us while letting our own call, our own wish, be? And what will then be the sign capable of signifying to each other the motive for which we have made our way in this direction?

Let us stop for a while at the threshold and the path. It is important that we might cross them in both directions; that is, that the return to our own dwelling, to ourselves, within ourselves, be secured. No doubt, we will return modified, but to come back home, to and within ourselves, is necessary. Taking shelter, gathering within the self are essential for the one who left one's own home, who ventured into spaces still unknown, who exposed oneself to the other, the foreigner or the stranger with regard to oneself. Only time, a space-time arranged in time, allows us not to appropriate these new regions, the call or the response of the other, and the traces left in us by this breaking out of our everyday dwelling. This does not mean that what attracted us outside is not more intimate than the intimacy that we have already experienced. But how to become familiar with such an appeal, coming from beyond us? How to prepare for it a memory and a becoming within ourselves?

All the more so since in order to respond, to correspond to it, we have to cross regions unknown to us but already marked with beacons, already populated, cluttered with past constructions: cultures, words, relationships. These regions are perhaps still virgin for us, but not in themselves. How can we make our way without getting lost: without forgetting the appeal, forgetting ourselves?

The path that brings us towards the other is not necessarily the one that leads us towards ourselves. Of course, if we have perceived the appeal, we have been called there where we already were. But that through which we are urged to leave our usual dwelling, that through which we are invited to respond, does not always correspond to the call that we have heard. A simple example: the other can appeal to me as mother, daughter or sister there where I felt myself appealed to as a lover. The meeting up of our paths towards one another is not ensured, and even less so the return of each one to one's own home. That through which we are moved by the words of the other is not necessarily that which is addressed to us as an appeal. Supposing that the other already knows the real intention of the call and the person to whom he, or she, wants to address it.

It is no longer a question of moving in a space arranged by the words of only one subject, but of taking the risk to open one's own world in order to move forward to meet with another world. Which constrains us, at each moment, to a double listening: to the language in which we already dwell, but also to the saying that the other addresses to us. Our coming into presence with one another can only happen through the intertwining of this double listening. Only this prepares a place in which we can approach one another.

Coming closer, once again, cannot amount to a simple spatial proximity in space or time, at least as categories defined more or less objectively, independently of the subjective life of each one. With regard to some aspects, however, spatio-temporal proximity has to be taken into account. For example, coming closer to the other can provide sensory apprehensions that our culture generally neglects or undervalues. Furthermore, perceiving through our eyes or through our ears does not obey the same temporal rhythms, and these rhythms are different again when we apprehend through our mind. It is the same for other senses, including touch itself, which had a share in this mysterious perception of the call, when we were still at home and had not yet met with the other.

How can we bring together and harmonize these various dimensions and rhythms of the encounter – in ourselves and between us? How can we place ourselves in relation to the appeal that we have perceived? How to respond, to correspond to it? Can wanting to do so with words be sufficient – even if they try to unite within them poetry and thought, thought and poetry? Is it not such a choice which has led us to lose the traces of the other in our human becoming?

Nevertheless, voice and words have to keep an important role, notably before and after the meeting. Our eyes alone could not recognize the other at the crossroads of our paths. The help of language will be essential, notably for remembering the intimate touch of the appeal. And the sound of the voice, with its musical modulations and its capacity for communing, must prepare an external and internal space where the coming into presence of the one and the other will be possible.

The place of meeting cannot be merely ecstatic with respect to our real surroundings, nor can it reduce itself to a sensible immediacy. In the words that each tries to say to the other, or that are said of the other, the bodies and the earthly dwelling where they live must resonate. No word can reach the rhythm, even less the melody, allowing one to approach the other – outside oneself or within oneself – if it comes from an already existing discourse. It even risks losing all meaning, and becoming a cradle not for life, for growth and love, but only for illusions and spells. Each time, speech must bring together, for each one and in each one, earth and sky, mortals and divinities. Entering into presence with one another requires that we say to the other and hear from the other at what point we have arrived in the approach and harmony between these parts of ourselves, without forgetting the ways in which they communicate or commune with the present regions of the universe in which we live. Which does not mean that they are simply common to us – we dwell differently in them. The other and myself do not have the same relation with these parts of ourselves and of the universe. Moreover, these polarities will lose their dichotomous pattern from the moment we assume, in ourselves, the becoming of their union and we enter into exchange through this becoming.

Of course, if one of us is supposed to be the heavens and similar to God while the other remains only earth and barely human, the different parts of the universe and of ourselves run the risk of becoming paralysed in their oppositions, indeed their conflicts. The heavens then seem to be able to exist independently from the earth, the divine from the human, the head from the body that animates thinking.

The atmosphere seems to be extraneous to the oceans and the plant world that produce it. And man, brought into the world by woman, claims to create her while forgetting his real beginning.

If each one cares for his or her own part of earth and sky, mortals and divinities, then approaching one another becomes possible. But in the dividing up of these polarities between the one and the other, within the one or within the other, coming closer remains impossible.

Words can, in each one and between the one and the other, bring together earth and sky, mortals and divinities, on the condition that they do not say one single truth and do not designate the world and things from a single perspective. In such a new approach, two polarities of a world, rather artificially defined, no longer try to become reunited, but exchange, with an alliance in view, two manners of dwelling in the world and in oneself. Listening becomes essential, but it alone cannot lead the way. To approach one another, a double listening is necessary. And it is the conjunction between the two listenings that can prepare the beginnings of a common dwelling.

If it is not so, that which is heard might only give voice to the one or the other, unless it were to belong to a saying grounded in a lack of consideration of the one or the other, and of their being in relation. Such a saying has dominated our discourses for centuries and it is difficult to overcome it so that we might hear what the other is saying to us, and even speak with ourselves without the screen of a language foreign to dialogue – that is to say, of a language that remains in a tautological logic of the same, in which it is difficult to say in the present what is to be said. The words are already dictated, substituting themselves for the one who tries to speak, speaking on one's own behalf. The subject would thus need to listen to what an already existing language enjoins it to say. Which perhaps has meaning when situating oneself in a world that is already there, but not for discovering a manner of saying to the other or of listening to what he, or she, has to say to us. About this, our tradition has seldom cared, striving instead to master living beings without being concerned about exchanging with them, indeed about receiving from them anything without any form of domination. This attitude is all the more harmful when the living world corresponds to the other part of humanity: woman. This part then remains torn between thing(s), nature and God without taking charge of what woman really is and what is proper to her.

In fact, what comes to face a speaking subject is another subject, and not only the horizon of a world that has been projected from a single discourse whose injunctions alone ought to be acknowledged. From what faces us, another language speaks to us, from beyond the world that we have appropriated. We need to listen to it, without relinquishing the discourse that is already ours. We need to listen without submitting ourselves or the other to a unique saying.

Our listening to words, and to what they have already established as nearness, in ourselves and around us, is thus questioned by the existence of other words, which again open the house of language in which we dwell. In such an event, and advent, what saying means is experienced. The practice of saying proves to be essential, and reveals that which is specifically human in it. It then gathers in its act all its dimensions: phonetic articulation, designation of things and of the world, expression of feelings, calling and listening, bringing close while maintaining remoteness, a search for harmony between earth and sky, mortals and divinities – in each one, between the two, in the world where they dwell. Language is thus confronted with the task that it has to assume as one proper to humans. But such a responsibility is still almost unknown to it. And that which has dominated its saying – the safeguarding of the same or Same – must be partially relinquished in order to approach the work that is really its work: to make human beings capable of saying.

This requires our being able to speak with the other and not only to name things and the world in which they take place. And this means entering into a new epoch of language, an epoch in which saying is no longer constituted in an ecstatic – ek-static – manner with respect to the real and its becoming. Thus an epoch in which the projection of the subject onto things and the world will not revert to the subject itself, both sheltering but also preventing this subject from meeting with the one who speaks other words and dwells in another world. Hence leading to the renunciation of a still open and living space and time that we could arrange for dialogue(s) in difference. If such a space and time are, even only ideally, rendered ecstatic in relation to the present by a previous establishment that is determined by a single and unique subject, then to speak with the other is impossible. There is only an already existing circle of discourse in which we must, each one, take up a place.

Such an ek-stasy of the real, cutting us off from the becoming of our growing, is not yet our real dwelling. If we cannot leave it, the encounter with the other as other remains inaccessible. We cannot experience it. The places of meeting, possible at the beginning, no longer exist. Of course, we may converse inside a horizon determined by the same – the Same. But this does not amount to experiencing what meeting with the other as other means, and what opening is required for such an event – or advent.

Giving up the ek-static closure of a world by a logic that secures its coherence through harmonization in the same, or Same, evokes the commentary of Stephan Georges' poem by Heidegger. There is, and there will be, no word for designating such a gesture. And a simple turning back will not allow us to discover it. To become aware of the circle in which I am, and to go around it, marking it with negativity with respect to the absolute, will remain a process or an act without words.

Does this then mean resignation? In a sense, yes. But accepting that I am not the whole also signifies the possibility of glimpsing a wider world, a greater completeness – that is, the possibility of overcoming a solitary destiny in order to be involved in a being-with-the-other that does not amount to a sharing of the same in the Same.

How to Welcome the Call of the Other?

Words from then on will have another status. It will no longer be a matter of having conversations or discussions with the other about a language already pronounced or still to be pronounced in the horizon of a supposedly common world. It will no longer be a matter of simply showing things to one another. What we have to speak, to say to each other, is not yet determined and will remain undetermined in a discourse existing outside us. Thus the first word we have to speak to one another is our capacity and acceptance of being silent. It would be the first wave of recognition addressed to the other as such. In this silence, the other may come towards me, as I may move towards him, or her. This silence is not strictly speaking a displaying – as, for example, when one shows to the other a flag of certain colours, sometimes white or black – but rather, or first of all, gives an indication concerning my ability to relinquish the meaning organized according to my signs and rules alone. It announces to the other that I keep a place, not only in myself to appropriate what is coming towards me, but also outside of myself in order to preserve a space and a time to let the one who is coming arrive.

The renunciation of speaking according to a discourse that we know in advance is a word of welcome to the one who comes to us from beyond the horizon that has been opened, but also closed, by our language. It is a welcoming to another world, to another manner of speaking and saying than the one we know. It is the laying out of a space-time that must still be virgin in order for a meeting to happen. What arrives, in fact, is not an event that already has a place in our own language. Welcoming cannot be reduced to a tone of voice, to a choice of kind words amongst all those that we use, unless we know how relative and insufficient this aspect is. Welcoming requires an availability for that which has not yet occurred, an ability and a wanting to open ourselves to the unknown, to that which is still unfamiliar to us and, in a sense, will always remain unfamiliar.

Welcoming does not take place simply in our dwelling, in ourselves, unless we arrange a space there which will never be ours, except as an availability on our part. Welcoming will first take place outside of us, even if this outside has a corresponding place within us and belongs to the most intimate part of ourselves. The welcome in ourselves, which we reserve for the other, is all the more non-appropriable since we accept the closeness of this other in ourselves. Since we try to receive the other there where we heard his or her call, in a part of ourselves that remains obscure to us, almost strange so that it seems inaccessible to us, although it constitutes the most intimate part of ourselves – that is, a place to which perhaps correspond words that do not intend to show, to make visible, and above all to demonstrate.

Such words are so strange to our culture because relations with the other have seldom been cultivated. Words which touch, stir, move or leave us waiting without reducing the event to a spectacular manifestation. Words which feed us without our assimilating them, making them our own, simply appropriating them. Words which approach without forcing the threshold, like a living element that comes from this side or beyond the limits of our dwelling. Such is the case for the light of the stars, the music of the wind, the song of the birds. They do not force us to do anything; rather they give assistance to our existence, put a surplus of life at our disposal, remind us of what or who we are. This happens on the condition that we do not intend to possess them, nor even to appropriate them through words, which remain always unable to express the energy, the life, that the light and music of the universe pass on to our perceptions, to the whole of ourselves.

To approach the other requires our trying to open a path that would not be first inspired by a showing or making appear. To make one's own way towards closeness does not here demand passing from the darkness of the night to the light of the day, but rather finding a manner of speaking which could be accompanied by a nocturnal luminosity. To turn our eyes towards the heart of the intimate risks undoing its touch – dividing, distinguishing, cutting off and thus isolating. Our eyes are not capable of seeing, nor even contemplating, intimacy, at least not directly. They can only imagine something about intimacy from the light, the gestures, the words that it radiates. But intimacy as such will remain invisible, irreducible to appropriation, and thus strange to the logic of Western discourse, to the logos, except in its delusion, its lack, its derelictions and artificial ecstasies. Intimacy allows itself neither to be seen nor to be seized. Nevertheless it is probably the core of our being. And any attempt to appropriate it risks annihilating being itself. However, it is not a question of magic, of irrationality, of madness – it is a question of touch.

And it is true that touch first arouses gesture: the gesture of going with respect and reverence towards its source, or the gesture of taking hold, of seizing. It is a gesture that will first respond to the call of the other.

In fact, it should be the gesture of going towards oneself in order to perceive whether someone, in us, could correspond to the call. Whether this call rings out in an emptiness where it resonates while becoming amplified, whether it awakens a flesh still unable to answer except by its own moving, or whether it goes to meet another call, proper to the one who receives it – that is, whether the call that has been heard corresponds to a call sent out or held in, so that the two could try to make their way towards one another and experience how they could listen to each other, approach one another, exchange with one another, enrich one another. The first gesture thus ought to be a listening to oneself or, more exactly, to the relation between that which touched us and that which we have in reserve for answering to this experience. It is a matter of listening to not merely an uttered word, which would be in search of its place in an already existing language to which the care of answering would be entrusted. If such were the case, language would be speaking with itself through us, continuing its age-old monologue.

The task before us is different: we need to be listening to a touch that perhaps already has a place in a discourse by which it has been appropriated or that remains silent, in some way virginal with respect to words. Virginal in an absolute sense, or touching again a space already appealed to but which has remained passive with respect to a possible response. Unless the first approach provoked only a withdrawal or an incorporation into our own body, our own horizon, without making the connection between what has been perceived and an other with whom it is fitting to meet.

The place where the call of the other reaches us ought to be unique. The one who sends it out is irreducible to anyone else and the circumstances of time and space are also singular. We are not prepared for this, in a way virginal, availability to the call of the other. Our culture has instead taught us to locate the other's fitting place in an already constituted meaning. In our own world, we could and even should, welcome the other in a place for guests, a room for guests. A space left vacant for the other would be preserved in ourselves and, above all, in our dwelling. But this space would be part of the very architecture of our world, of our subjectivity. It would represent a sort of space for hospitality, which would be neutral or indifferent with respect to the one who is calling to us.

We are not yet then really available to the call of the other. This other occupies a space built for any other, outside of our being reached within ourselves and being questioned in the present. There where we offer hospitality to the other, we are already absent. We welcome or shelter the other because of some political-cultural paternalism or maternalism, some social idealism or ideology, some religious or moral commandment. But this welcome that we give to the other is not really addressed to him or her, and does not let them really be free.

It is not in some immutable dwelling in which we have reserved a place for just any guest that we must welcome the one who is calling us. The place in which we could welcome this other is still to be discovered, to be opened, to be arranged. It is important to feel and to listen with the whole of who we are there where we have been reached by the appeal, and to how we should respond to this being touched. No doubt, to give traditional hospitality is better than completely closing off one's own home to the other. But this does not yet amount to a sharing with the other. Unless we limit it to a material level, which preserves the possibility of arriving at desire by protecting life itself for the one who maintains the difference between need and desire.

To respond to the call of the other at the level of needs is more generous than simply closing one's door, but we are not yet really called into question other than at the level of having. With regard to Being, it is another matter, one having to do precisely with desire. If our desire confines itself to a will for immutability, for permanence of self-identity, for the security of dwelling in sameness, for the perfection of a self-ideal, our desire remains closed to welcoming the other as other. Then one can only keep the other outside oneself, outside one's world, one's horizon, whatever the space that would be reserved for this other in one's own country, one's own city or home, indeed one's own bed, and whatever may be the bread shared. There is not yet a sharing of Being, which presupposes opening oneself to a becoming to which we agree to be attentive, to listen. Not merely an individual becoming in a horizon already defined by a culture, a language, a people. But a human becoming that calls into question what has already happened to humanity, and that allows and clears the way for new perspectives on Being, with new obligations and possibilities for human blossoming.

It is only at such a price that we can prepare a welcome for the other, whomever this other could be: a companion, a friend, a child, a foreigner. It is always a question of how to become capable of being with the other, and of making a new world, a third world, exist between us.

If our hospitality confines itself to offering a place or a room for guests, it is because we are not yet able to do better. We offer to the other that which we unconsciously reserve for ourselves: an enclosed space partly defined around a void. The place that we give to the other in fact amounts to a representation of the place that we ourselves occupy – a space apparently open in a closed world. As far as we are concerned, we cannot perceive the place in which we live, because it is cluttered with our objects, our projections, our repetitions, our habits and tautologies. It is both enclosed and partly cluttered with our own emptiness.

We offer to the other a part of this enclosed and, in some way, empty, territory – a sort of prison cell, in fact like our own. To be sure, the other will be sheltered, but in an enclosed space, a place already defined by our norms, our rules, our lacks and our voids. The other will have the possibility of dwelling only in a loop of the interlacing of relations where we ourselves are situated by our culture, our language, our surroundings. Blind to our lack of freedom.

Moreover, do we not strive to save a place for the other hoping, more often than not unconsciously, that the other will put an end to our confinement, create a draught of air in our enclosed and saturated world? Will not an other, apparently staying outside and without any shelter, be the one who will reopen our world? Hence the gesture of welcoming him or her, indeed of making them guests of honour. No doubt in an ambiguous way.

Sharing Needs, Sharing Desire

But there is not yet in this an answer to the call of the other, except sometimes at the level of material needs. Even at this level, we often share with the belief that this will be given back to us in one way or another, even if only through the superior feeling that we experience – which is unconscious for most of us. Hegel was not wrong in condemning pity, the support of a status quo maintained by some masters in our human becoming, and in fact another name for contempt. We often give in order to receive, not necessarily from an other, but rather as an effect of our gesture upon ourselves – to feel greater, more open and noble. Thus our gesture does not really address the other. Most of the time, we have not yet perceived that the other exists as such. If this were the case, perhaps we would hesitate to take an interest in him or her, ignoring what could happen to us. The other, it is true, is beyond our horizon. To address him, or her, means to agree to question this horizon – thus to risk the loss of our shelter, a shelter that is not only material but also cultural or spiritual. We accept this risk with difficulty, our tradition having generally forbidden us from doing that. Thus we sometimes transform a material sharing into a spiritual value. The other becomes an opportunity for making personal spiritual progress or benefits, that we imagine to be shareable – but with a God or in God, rather than with the other here and now present at our side.

It is true that sharing the spiritual is not a simple matter – unless we entrust all our progresses and profits to a community. But this often amounts to annihilating that which is most personal to us and to binding together, and even fixing, the community with that which ought to be the most precious leaven for our personal becoming. For lack of having discovered, or invented, the gestures, the words, the acts that are suitable for this personal spiritual becoming, capable of keeping it and ensuring its ground, we sacrifice it in a form of common energy. Then the lack of an appropriate differentiation makes our spiritual dimension regress because of an adhesion to a faith or to a group. Of course, this adhesion can sometimes be of some help. It represents nevertheless, with regard to the perception of a living transcendence that keeps the mind or the soul awake and on the way, a double risk of becoming stuck or bogged down: in already established truths and in relations with the other(s) determined by them.

Spiritual community itself is not without danger. If a personal spiritual becoming ought to go hand in hand with respect for what already exists or could exist, if it remains open with its progress in view, the same seldom goes for a community. The issues there are often already fixed and rigid, having become sorts of imposed dogma that transform the frailty of a personal spiritual energy into an artificially affirmative, and even repressive, force.

What had to remain not fixed, a sort of sap for becoming, gets lost. The flesh and breath, mainspring and ground of our evolution, are forgotten to the advantage of almost warlike proclamations that speak more to possible enemies than say what the matter is, in this moment, regarding our perception of transcendence. We affirm a faith that binds us together, that makes us a people. And we then often give up a personal quest that is always risky, always uncertain, always still to be discovered, to be paved. Transcendence is presented to and imposed on us as a sort of object or objectivity, kept out of reach to ensure its inaccessibility to our sensible and even mental perceptions. Transcendence no longer requires us to accomplish a movement of withdrawing, of respecting and waiting towards an other who is irreducible to us and from whom some teaching, some favour could come. Swearing allegiance to already uttered words is presented to us as the way towards the transcendent, which then evades our approach – already past, never present or future. Such an issue, the most crucial in order to make our way towards that which always remains beyond our grasp, is imposed on us as already defined; which does not favour, to say the least, an awakening that attracts us to itself, that gets us on the way towards it. And that constrains us to become beyond that which already is: both within us and outside of us.

Always already defined, the other has to become absolute in order to remain irreducible to our grasp. The other is no longer transcendent because he or she is different from us, but because otherness has been postponed until another world, beyond our horizon as mortals. And there are often already defined procedures that are supposed to lead us to the Other, but which make this Other inaccessible. We are separated from such an Other by words, by gestures that are to be repeated without us really perceiving their meaning. And this strengthens the status of a presumed transcendence, even if there were to be nothing beyond the path that ought to lead us to it. A path that risks removing us from rather than bringing us closer to a perception of what could be the transcendental. We find ourselves then separated from the other and from ourselves, having moreover lost the feeling that is able to conduct us towards one another, as well as the energy essential to realize such a journey. Thus, we are both enclosed, the one and the other, in spaces surrounded by strongholds and at the same time mixed together without any real alterity having been recognized. The other has become our Other. But this has to remain unrepresentable as truth; hence the importance of obstacles constructed in order to isolate us from one another.

We are simultaneously inside one another, or rather both merged in the same, and confronted with insurmountable boundaries that make the Same inaccessible. We are thus deprived of the possibility of envisioning what governs us, and divided within ourselves between a part that we have to command and another, the most subtle and creative part, which ought to blindly submit to the command of that which remains foreign to it even though being the Same, at least for a part of humanity. What availability is left to us to welcome the other, here and now, if we are in this way reduced to one part that obeys duties and habits, and another part that is waiting for an inaccessible transcendence whose agents, they too, subject access to duties and habits? What free energy have we at our disposal for such a gesture, in the present and the future? Where will we find the strength, the space and the time for accomplishing it, for being faithful to it? Unless perhaps in an empty room, outside or within us, waiting for the other to submit to the same and the Same, on pain of being rejected, expelled.

We have not then begun to welcome the other, to correspond to his, or her, call. At best, we postpone this call until another world, in this way failing to care for the most human dimension of ourselves: relating to the other as other – that is, with respect for our difference(s).

Having relations with the same, at a natural or cultural level, does not represent a really human task. To be sure, one could argue here that it belongs to humans to respect the boundaries of their species, but such respect should be a way of becoming aware of the difference inside this species. Humanity cannot define itself only through its opposition to other species, an opposition that, moreover, it transposes between the different parts which compose it. Rather, it must distinguish itself by another manner of dealing with difference(s).

Approaching the other, as far as humans are concerned, should not be submission to blind instinct – sexual attraction and possession, reproduction, subjection, appropriation, rejection, etc. – but the perception of our humanity as such; that is, access to that which transcends us, with regard to which silence, listening and words are tasks that are incumbent on us here and now. Not as a repetition of behaviours, notably linguistic ones, that we already know, but rather as an experience of a saying for which we are responsible. Through such a gesture, we become humans, women and men assuming their nature with a relational perspective that is different from that of the plant or animal kingdoms.

This demands that we be able to listen to our attractions, and also to contain them, in order to prepare a space between us where desire could be fulfilled through entering into dialogue.

Some passages in this chapter first appeared in 'The Path towards the Other' in *Beckett after Beckett*, ed. S. E. Contarski and A. Uhlmann (University of Florida Press, 2006), 39–51.

At the Crossroads – the Encounter

The Event – or Advent

Something has happened – an event, or an advent – an encounter between humans. A breath or soul has been born, brought forth by two others. There are now three living beings for whom we lack the ways of approaching, the gestures and words for drawing nearer to one another, for exchanging.

Something exists, is there. But what? Perhaps nothing that could respond or correspond to such a question. Nevertheless, it is important to care for this newborn – in each one, between the two. Three births alter the one, the other, the whole. No doubt we perceive them, but we do not know how to be concerned with them. We are touched, filled with wonder, but disconcerted.

We also worry about the failing, indeed the death, of these germs of life, impetuous but delicate, wanting to grow but still in need of being sheltered – in the one, in the other, and between the two. There are now at least three new existences, which, at this very moment, make us pass from one life to another, from one world to another.

Coming back within ourselves, closer to our centre, but unfamiliar with this heart of ourselves where we now are; unknown to ourselves, as is unknown to us the one who brought us into this most intimate place, as well as what we have thus created without having really decided to do so. How could we want that of which we have not the slightest idea? That which happens by itself because a single gesture has taken place.

A gesture – and all is, or appears, different. So much so that one gets lost, even in one's own world, and one no longer perceives as such what was once familiar. The tactile nature of the environment seems to be changed. And the desire to take refuge or coil up does not make the slightest difference. The weaving of the surroundings has become other, and a shelter can no longer be found. The outside is in part turned inside? Because someone intervened in the environment that formed a body or flesh with oneself. In fact, it is not only that. The flesh itself is no longer the same. It is moved by surges, by flows, by appeals, which risk tearing apart its weaving. It overflows with a surplus and suffers from voids. It is permeated by joys, but also by anxieties, by excess and lack in relation to the present, to presence. A presence that seems to have remained with the other – or to be suspended between the two. And which it is not easy to bring back to oneself. Supposing that one wants to, and that such a wish would not be in vain.

Something has happened. How could I deny this, or want to nullify its having taken place? And, moreover, why? Unless I find in it an obstacle in my way, an impossible crossroads upon my path, a disowning of myself. But this does not seem to be the case. Except, of course, in the strangeness of what is experienced, the uncertainty regarding the becoming – of myself, of the other, of that which has been born between the two. Three newborns who must be cared for, without knowing how.

Due to a lack of being able to understand, is it perhaps necessary to begin by cultivating what has happened, or happens, to oneself? At least, to try. This means to accept, to welcome and to preserve the existence and the growth of what has occurred, without neglecting or throwing out of balance one's own journey. Thus avoiding an excessive opening or withdrawal. Maintaining a possible rhythm of one's heart? Harmonized with the rhythm of the earth? Which already safeguards life itself. Caring for it first.

Any mutation involves a sort of death. And the risk is greater yet when it is a matter of a sharing that calls into question the whole self, that interrupts the way itself. No doubt this way will have to again be taken. But without a radical questioning of one's solitary journey, meeting with the other is impossible. Nevertheless, it is important to remain faithful to one's own journey. Otherwise no perspective on the encounter will be possible, and its becoming will prove to be impossible.

What happens is extra-ordinary, super-human, wonderful and terrific. Which explains why this event has always been unrecognized, denied, avoided. For example, by making of the other a part of oneself, by dividing humanity into two poles, by reducing the union of these two poles to a return to mere naturalness. Thus man would search, with nostalgia and repulsion, in woman for his own repressed and uncultivated natural pole. And this would prevent woman from truly being an other for him, and their meeting from reaching a cultural or spiritual dimension. Unless they have recourse to some divinity or to a horizon of parental sublimation? Hindering, once more, the advent of the between-two from happening. The space is already mapped out, pre-occupied. Thus, what could come to pass, as a result of a new event, will not happen. It is already invested in or projected onto some transcendence or some natural child – a proof that something took place, a tangible result of a union. Of which the reality is both evident and problematic, irrefutable and enigmatic, very moving and evanescent. How to be sure that a union has occurred – which presupposes the one, the other and the between-two?

Would the grace of an encounter, when it happens, be that I know what the other feels? Of course, I do not know, in a speculative way that can be set out and argued. Rather, I experience a more comprehensive, intimate and mysterious knowledge. The encounter, if it took place, has generated this knowledge in me. And the doubt, then, would only be the result of a mental alienation because of a too abstractly logical culture, or an egocentric quibbling which might annihilate such a knowledge. Before carrying any child, I carry the other in myself: you-me in me. I am in some way pregnant with your desire, your love, your soul. Which lifts me up rather than weighing me down.

But this also endangers my life. My centre of gravity is no longer the same: less physical or differently physical. The body and the soul have become inseparably united, whereas before they were more separated. The psyche and the spiritual are from now on carnal. Which modifies their density, their weight.

But to attain, in an instant, another equilibrium, is no simple matter. And such a transformation of my own experience renders uncertain each of my gestures, my words, my decisions. How can I deal with this I, this me, whom I do not know? How to preserve their life, and protect them from being merged with what happened in the encounter, with what is perceived of the other, or of me-the other? How to set off again along the way after this sudden transformation of energy? Which occurred in myself, no doubt, but thanks to a synergy with the other. A synergy that I could not provoke or reproduce alone and as I please, but of which I keep the perception and which I still remember, at least for the time being. My blood, my breath are still suspended at the crossroads where we were, even if only for a short moment, two in one. And each one in each one, each in oneself, but also other. How to deal with this other, her and even him, whom I have seemingly become? Which was only possible because I was different, because I could meet with, marry, carry in myself the other. On the condition that I remain myself.

In a natural conception, the relations between the one who carries and the one who is carried are regulated without a particular decision. They even resolve the question of the difference of the sexes between mother and child. We perhaps favour a physical begetting in love because of its easiness. The psychic or spiritual work is really less difficult in this case than in the encounter between man and woman, especially between lovers. An unconscious dishonesty then leads us to overvalue genealogical relations to the detriment of love as such. Is it not most important in our culture to master the situation in which we find ourselves, thus nature itself, the world, the other? But such behaviour proves to be impossible in love. And emphasizing eroticism to the detriment of love, under the cover of sexual liberation, amounts to a new way of evading the task that awaits us – at the crossroads.

It is a specifically human task. Indeed, it is divine and not diabolic as our tradition has often claimed, thereby risking to lead us into mistaking the other, at least the different other, with the devil – which our culture has also insinuated. Hence the status of woman, and of the foreigner?

No doubt, opening one's own journey in order to welcome the other as other at the crossing of our paths is not without risk: of losing one's way, of seeing any subtlety in energy vanish or disappear, of reducing transcendence to the facticity of an encounter, of getting lost in the other or wanting to possess this other. Which would be physically difficult, even if the confinement of women in the house partially had such a meaning. At a psychic or mental level, who does not try to appropriate the other, even if only unconsciously? Has God himself not served as a means of appropriating the other, of annihilating his, and above all her, difference? Without yet speaking of our logic founded upon the attempt to abolish the difference between the two gendered parts of humanity, thus to nullify any real alterity.

The other does not thus exist for us, except as something more or less than ourselves: greater or smaller, more powerful or more destitute, a parent or a child. The other then represents an alteration of ourselves, for better or for worse, someone who is valued according to the same criteria as our own identity, a same assigned to an index more or less. Together we are not two; at best, we sometimes enter into the composition of a great unity: humanity, people, family … As long as we are not able to emerge from such totalities, we are never in front of one another, beside one another, with one another.

Now, something like this has happened, at least for me. At least, I perceived it in this way. What I said ought to take place has occurred. At the crossroads: an other – the encounter. Both an obstacle and an opening. A radiating black, seemingly nothing – a radical stopping and a return to a fullness.

I could imagine that what hinders my journey there is a body. I could imagine that a body stands across my path, my life. That it is a question of a body, only a body. And, with this body, all the taboos, the mysteries, the opacity that a culture has projected onto it. Hence, the amazement, the hesitation, the exultation that are felt when approaching it, as well as the entry into darkness that accompanies this gesture. The intimidation too that one senses, an intimidation that one sometimes tries to exorcize through an erotic arrogance which solves nothing. Instead, it abolishes the discovery, and annihilates what sprang from it. While intending to prevail by force or ruse over this young growth, it destroys what gave birth to it in ourselves. The yet-nothing, a kind of resisting totality with which we were confronted, becomes a no-longer-anything. The flesh, born from the encounter, then only leaves an emptiness after being reduced to an energy to be mastered, to be exhausted in order to put an end to the obstacle, the questions, the overflow and the absence, the jubilation and the anxiety.

In order to return to the homeostasis of a solitary energy, to a daily little death, to a making outside ourselves that is inattentive to ourselves, to a disappearance of ourselves in the construction of a collective temple dedicated to a defunct humanity.

What we had furtively unveiled to one another, through the approach between us, is annihilated, forgotten, erased from our humanity – of which we became the murderers. We are the unconscious murderers of ourselves. Hence a survival hanging on to some hope, disguised in various ways, of a future in which life would finally be.

We are waiting for a life dependent on an Other for lack of having cared for that life born in the meeting with the other, here and now. This delicate new life is then sacrificed to some omnipotent divinity instead of being cradled between us as a giving birth to ourselves. A birth whose imperceptible envelopment must be unceasingly generated by our care, and not extrapolated onto the self-sufficient totality of an Absolute including each one and that which occurred between us. Triply unsheltered, we are searching in some Other for guarantees of our existence, for parameters to substitute for a vanishing identity, for an unlimited verticality in order to disguise the in-finite of our being in presence. We direct our breath, our soul, towards some God, brought back in this way to the mortal finitude of our bodies in order to escape the vertigo arising from what is revealed to us. We are thus torn apart between the higher and the lower, another crossroads covering over, eluding, the crossroads where we are situated – a horizontal one, but one that gathers all dimensions. On the condition that we are attentive, patient, enduring; that we are cautious and without fear. On the condition that we are alert but quieted enough to welcome what arrives – the other who happens to us in darkness, in the abandon of a half-sleep. Outside any mastery, any seizure, by whatever sense. The other who, imperceptibly, becomes himself in myself – us. Without this having truly been decided or willed.

Only for a Moment, Sharing the Home

How can I know what will result from a gesture? To which I agreed. Thus accepting to expose myself – to the other. And to an encounter of which I had only a premonition, without imagining that, even if only for a moment, we would become two in one. Although she who said 'yes' knew that something like this had already taken place. Otherwise, why this 'yes'? But to sense in a confused manner the existence of a call, of a welcome, of a given confidence, and to try to correspond to them through faithfulness to a word, does not yet amount to finding oneself in front of an explicit demand of the other. No doubt all this has made possible such a demand, imperceptibly preparing a space where it could be heard.

It was not, for all that, perceived as such. Hence the question – and the 'yes'. As well as this setting for a human encounter that we have built in an instant, and in which we dwelled together. Becoming two in one thanks to it? Leaving our respective homes to run the risk of exposing ourselves to the other, with the other, within the other inside a shared space.

Apparently this place has immediately been left. Yet it is unforgettable in fact, because it has passed from an outside to an inside. Where it will not be easily deconstructed. This has taken place – for ever. Unless we abandon our humanity, and in particular the link between body and word(s) which establishes it. A link for which it is necessary to be two.

A link that we have, in an instant, re-tied. Establishing or restoring human being between us. So that this newborn, which we have brought into the world, is ours, and more. It is a child of the human element, the seed of humanity – born of an exchange of word(s) and flesh between us. It is a real different from all that has been taught to us about reality. Nevertheless, it is there if we consent to pay attention to it, as a care more important for humanity than allegiance to any already defined law or right, to which we, the one and the other, ought to submit. Indeed, it is no longer a matter of ensuring a little more order among individuals assimilated to some people or herd who obey precepts imposed upon them from outside. Rather it is a question of returning to the elementary duties that can bind us to and with one another as humans – a wedding between body and word(s) that each must both secure as one's own in the present and expose to a meeting with the other. A wager, a risk, an assent that, for a moment, relinquish reflection and withdrawal, agreeing that, at the crossroads, an encounter take place, the work or impact of which it is not possible to foresee if the two in it really abandon themselves to one another, without exactly knowing who is the one and who is the other. Both obeying an appeal that, in part, exceeds them, even if they are its source and its vehicle, an appeal that they must let be until this abandon of oneself to the other.

Such an abandon seems to be an end, beyond which it is not possible to go and from which it is not possible to come back. It has thus been extrapolated into God: a dark end towards which we move as towards the Absolute, beyond which is nothing, and into which each loses oneself for ever. An Absolute that helps us to evade the task which is incumbent on us regarding the relation to the other – who, at the crossroads, is waiting for us. An other from whom it will be necessary to come back to ourselves, whatever of ourselves has been risked in him, or her. An other who does not indefinitely move back before our approach, who sometimes is there and with whom it could happen that we meet, returning then to ourselves and to a journey of which the end is now modified – in suspense, hidden, still imperceptible. Nevertheless, it is advisable to continue along the path, even if no oral or written law has already paved it.

Only the memory of a word, of an experience remains, and a faithfulness necessary for one to avoid chaos, destruction, dereliction, the loss of one's way. But this faithfulness is to something indistinct, without any form on which one's attention could be focused. It is only a trace within oneself, a denseness, a temperature, a tone that lingers or vanishes according to some act or other being carried out, some thought being cultivated, some meeting taking place. The reality here is both fleeting and more vivid than many other obvious facts. But the loyalty towards it is complex, all the more complex since it is difficult to distinguish what, in it, belongs to the one or to the other. Furthermore, does such a question have meaning? Is it not necessarily to the two that this reality refers? How to be faithful to the two at once? Is it not the one who perceives this conjunction who has to be faithful, even if only to bring the other back to it? While letting this other make his or her own way, a way for which markers are missing? How can we then carry out such a gesture while letting the other be as other? While letting this other carry out their own journey? Even if they grow remote, forget, indeed lose themselves. Who will bring this other back to the place of the encounter, of which nothing remains in them? If, for example, he, for his part, is pregnant with no child? If his relation to time, his memory are different from mine? If, in a way, he does not remember? Is it a matter of unveiling to him what could ensure the existence of the two? Of affirming that I have a responsibility towards the subsistence and the growth of this two, these two, and what was born of them? Or of trusting what, in the other, has been engendered and remains, requiring a return to take place? At a rhythm that, perhaps, differs from mine. Supposing that I know it, and that it has not become so modified that I have to reinvent a rhythm in order that life continue – an indispensable condition for being faithful ...

It is perhaps to her, as living nature, that I have to abandon myself in order to preserve my own life, its growth, and what they bear of the life and growth of the other. Such a hospitality is so subtle and intimate that I have to seek help in nature for my survival and my becoming, notably through being attentive to the abundance that she gives to be contemplated, heard, breathed, touched, felt. It suffices to agree to receive, in silence, this eucharist that she unsparingly offers – often without any visible object or symbol but as a communion with the real presence of the living. No transubstantiation is necessary here – life itself is there, giving itself through all that surrounds me. On the condition that I stop for a while and consent to this gift.

Which does not go, later, without mourning. What or who could be equivalent to such a profusion of bliss?

And how to harmonize this happiness with the one experienced with him, the other? How to go from the one to the other, faithful to the two, without having to relinquish being with the one or with the other, within the one or within the other?

Unless the order of the things become reversed here – being in nature, I bear the other within me. I would need to be enveloped by her to be able to keep him in myself. Thus he would be sheltered and fed by nature through me, who consents to such a viaticum in order to protect, within me, this foreign presence. A presence that I desire and must preserve without knowing how, and without knowing what will come of it. For example, at what time things might be reversed – her vanishing in him who, in turn, will envelop me. And what happiness and uncertainty will accompany such a passage, and the entry into a different duration, of which the rhythm and the unfolding now depend on the other. That is to say, on a will and a desire that I do not know, and will never master – on pain of the encounter no longer taking place. Nor this reversal of her in him, who, at times, envelops me. Condensing in such a gesture the whole of her? Embodying, for a moment, an unlimited life in order to make him present to me, with me. Which is not without the mystery, the enthusiasm and the reserve, but also the risk, that inspire such a human, and more than human, gesture. We were, we are, two.

But is this not always what is at stake with human being? Without being two, does human being really exist? And all that has already occurred to humanity, is it something

43

other than making the way towards such a crossroads – the encounter?

But meeting cannot happen from the very beginning nor from time immemorial. It is necessary to have been one in order to become two. The childhood of the little human being is actually longer than has been asserted. It cannot stop with the aptitude for satisfying in an autonomous way one's own needs; it requires knowing desire and being able to share it. We have not stopped shirking this specifically human task. And whatever the age of humanity itself, we still know almost nothing about it; indeed it is not even certain that we have not regressed on the way to such a human accomplishment. Which appears to us as an impassable threshold, beyond which we could not go.

Is this not still what happens to us today after our encounter? We have crossed the threshold, and we have thus lost our bearings. Except that a happiness, a warmth, a strength exist in us that we do not really know how to preserve, to adjust, or to harmonize with what was experienced by each before our becoming two in one? If only for a fleeting instant.

I am here assuming that the same occurred to the two. Differently no doubt. But even if this happened only to me, how could I take on its meaning, be faithful to it, favour its becoming? No doubt there exists a meaning, but it is so different from the meaning taught to us that we are blind to it. With what sight, moreover, ought we to perceive it? It is in darkness that we met with one another. Scarcely having built a rudimentary common dwelling – thanks to a few words – we entered into the night.

A night that we did not leave. Could it be through my

own doing? How could I know this? We left each other without any word, any look or other gesture. Divided without a return to the two, without a sign that signalled the crossing by each one of the threshold of our shared dwelling. Improvised, almost in the middle of the day, in the public arena of a great city, of which I could not say whether it was busy or empty.

When, finally, I turned round to wave to the other, there was no longer anyone to whom to direct a sign. This neither surprised nor saddened me. Afterwards, I began to wonder and even held myself a little to blame. But I do not really believe in this guilt on my part. What words, what signs, were possible when we were emerging from this moment of night? Would they not have inevitably ruined the imprint sealed in one instant but forever, and which will require a very long time, perhaps a life or an eternity, to be deciphered and obtain the respect and the attention that it merits?

There is nothing here that resembles the visible sign designated as a symbol; that is, an object divided into two parts, of which each of us keeps one in order, one day, to meet again by bringing the two parts together. It is our encounter that formed an imprint, and an invisible seal between us. Certainly our memory keeps a few traces of this, but it cannot, for all that, show us how to reconstitute such a seal. Only the appeal to the other will be of help, and the perception of what has happened. But how then to distinguish what comes from me and what comes from the other? What needs to be cultivated in a withdrawal into the self and what can exist only thanks to the presence of the other.

A presence that could only happen at some other crossroads, after each has again travelled the path towards oneself, within oneself. After each has experienced what occurred in the meeting, and whether this could, indeed must, take place again, in order to be faithful to oneself, to the other, to the difference between the two. To draw the other onto one's own path or to let oneself go astray on the path of the other would indeed amount to suppressing the appeal and making it impossible for a seal to be formed again. This one will be both more complex and simple than the first – a faithfulness has already modified its imprint, sealing and opening certain possibilities.

From Familiarity to Intimacy

A between-us already exists – which unites us, forces us to be faithful, and frees us from a confinement: in ourselves, in a tradition or a community. An opening has been created in the horizon of a personal or collective world, which puts the limits of such a world into perspective. We have crossed its closure and, from then on, we are without any cover but already linked, in a way, by other commitments that we undertook by ourselves, without really knowing where they would lead us, and which take root deeper or higher than the foundations to which we were accustomed. We are henceforth emancipated from a familiar environment, uprooted to another world for which we still lack gestures, images, words, even if this world is more intimately ours and we ventured to enter it driven by a necessity that was our own. Now this is not always the case with the culture in which we have been situated without any decision on our part, and in which we conform to experiences made by others that, little by little, exile us from ourselves or mould our identity in a way irrelevant to us but of which we become prisoners.

We are confirmed in this losing of our way by the fact that the same goes for all those who surround us, who are as strange to themselves as we are to ourselves – thus incapable of taking us back to our real. This real that, in our encounter, was present, at least partly. Otherwise, a crossroads would not have existed, nor an event or advent. Nor the formation of a between-us, born, including within ourselves, from those who we were. A between-us for which we must care, like for some star, some prophecy, some announcement being the sign of a new horizon, new progressions and ways of Being that will introduce us, alone or together, into a world until now unknown. Nevertheless, this world is more our own than what we lived as familiarity itself.

But we advance in darkness, and without the environment of known settings and objects that we confuse with familiarity. A familiarity that then amounts to an external proximity to things, and even to others, to which we entrust the most intimate part of ourselves without ever approaching it. Which moves us far away from ourselves, and makes meeting with the other impossible – an other who has disappeared into the world that surrounds us or has been expelled from this world, which their mere presence questions, undoes, breaking the proximity of things and of people to themselves and to us. But such a proximity is not really nearness; it is frozen in space and repetitions, not alive in the present, and is maintained by already defined rules and imperatives rather than by a faithfulness that needs to be invented each time.

In our crossroads, this sort of familiarity broke up – no doubt a familiarity that was not very accomplished, but which nevertheless ensured some coherence and order in our everyday life, the confinement of which a gap towards the sky allowed us to endure, without too much anxiety.

The weaving of a familiar world is henceforth undone. And I am left in some way naked in strange surroundings. In myself, a different certainty is born that nourishes me with a new life. It is no longer a known environment that accompanies my everyday activities at each moment, but instead a secret inner reality that gives a rhythm to my breathing, to the flow of my blood, to the tempo of my gestures, to the choice of my words. Something unknown governs me from the most intimate core of myself, something that does not appear to my senses or my knowledge, yet is unquestionably there, more present to me than any other presence. As long as I make time to pay attention to what so animates my breath, my heart, my way of moving and saying – in a manner that sometimes surprises me. As does what I ignored of myself, and has been unveiled in this advent. Indeed, it is not some external pressure that compels me to some change or other. It is from inside myself that the inspiration or obligation comes. Not like those aroused by a child with whom I would be pregnant, but like those coming from a new breath, a new soul that the other has given or revealed to me, and which are not without relations with his, or hers. If this were not the case, an encounter would not have taken place, but rather an acting or engendering by the other within me, and not a union between us. A union in which it was not possible, at least for a moment, to say who was the one and who was the other, and even less to say what is the nature of that to which we have given birth in us, and between us.

To take on the responsibility towards this meeting is so difficult, which is not to say painful, that we will attempt various ways of evading it. For example, we will reduce the other to the same as a something or a someone already known – which nullifies the event, or advent. Are the words that have been said not the same as those an other, a few years ago, already pronounced? Could it be a question of an unconscious appropriating repetition by the one who recently addressed them to me? With a better way of listening on my part? Was a time of deafness to the words of the other necessary so that, this time, they acquired their whole value and echoed within me, allowing the building of a home where we dwelled together? Notably thanks to the attention that I paid to my own words in response to those of the other.

The schema of a dialogue might then be used as a framework for the place in which we met together – the same words that were pronounced a few years ago not having succeeded in ensuring such a function. But am I not here giving in to the temptation to jeopardize an advent, that has now become possible, through questions about anteriority or precedence, and, in this way, to nullify its present nature – that is, the entry into presence of the other? Why am I doing so? Because of a fear of this event? Because of a concern to give to each his or her due? Because of wanting to find my own way again? These three motives, and even more, probably intertwine. But such questions break into the act of the encounter, dismantle its unity, nullify its occurrence. Was not the paradoxical result of our meeting to bring us back to ourselves? To gather together each in oneself thanks to an opening to the other as other, which requires holding onto oneself, and also thanks to the gesture of the other assenting to the one who I am.

The welcome given to and by the other is what returns us to ourselves. Only this gesture gives back to each one his or her own self in its entirety – with its own borders, world and horizon. This presupposes that we are two, and two who are different. Otherwise all forms of inclusion or exclusion, incorporation or objectification, fragmentation or dilution, etc. are at work. Whereas when we are really two, each one can gather the other without any instrument or object, through one's presence alone. A presence which, with a gesture or sometimes a few words, gives back to the other the presence that is proper to them.

Through such a gift, which each offers to the other as a result of recognizing him, or her, as other, we are both two and one. Each has to be oneself and return to oneself in one's otherness in order for unity to exist – as a seal between immanence and transcendence that the one and the other share but which can be sealed only between the two.

In this sealing, bodies take part, bodies in some way innocent and not perverted by a culture which assigns to them functions different from those of being a mediation in relational life. When we neglect, indeed ignore, this dimension of the body, our body becomes a mere tool of production at the service of our individual or collective needs or powers. It no longer ensures the specifically human mediation that desire requires. A desire which, as such, founds humanity and its becoming, and cannot be reduced to the cause of its decline or decay, as has too often been said and practised in the West. A desire which establishes links between humans, and at first between two of them. For lack of starting still and always from two, what unites human beings tends to become a more or less abstract collective energy, quite similar to the animal energy of a horde or a herd, and which may fall into all sorts of authoritarian or totalitarian deviancies. Since it is not adjusted at each moment by the mutual desires of the one and the other, the energy is accumulated, capitalized on, and one forgets its source and its aim, against which one turns it, ruining the relation from which it was born. Desire then becomes enslavement, possession, cancellation of the other. Its meaning was to create links between two different subjectivities, but it now annihilates such a distinction instead of respecting and cultivating it.

Such care cannot be entrusted to words alone, above all to already existing words, words not appropriate to the specific situation where desire arises, to the two subjects between whom desire exists. Words are to be invented. But words are too often already separated from the body in which desire originates, and are thus always separating us from it, from ourselves. Nevertheless, they are essential for outlining the dialogic structure of the encounter, for building a setting where the two will be present. Words are thus necessary, but so is all that which will support the sensible existence of each one in the relations between the two – which requires a sensory attention to the other.

To what would entering into presence be reduced if this attention is lacking? To the abstract violence of a blind force? Without the adjustments and harmonies that are indispensable for the existence of a between-two respectful of each one. Which calls on us to embody the attraction in seeing, listening, touching, and even breathing, tasting.

The encounter brightens in such a light, whatever the part of night that binds me to the other. But the space and the time of the appeal are not only entrusted to a nocturnal path, they also have to organize the scene of the entry or the return into presence. Which cannot amount to somehow appearing: the other is revealed, little by little, to me, in this way soothing the aspiration or anxiety that I feel. A gesture appeases my eyes, stopping to observe, to contemplate or to recollect the manifestation of a presence. An incantation of the voice, a phrasing or a rhythm in speaking, a choice of words hold my listening attentive to the particular one who is expressing himself or herself. A fragrance invites me to take time to breathe in and enjoy it, to impregnate my memory with it while letting be, in the present, the link that it establishes between the two.

But this between-two also needs to be inhabited by a bilateral scenography of performance made up of words, voices, gestures. No doubt each one has to present to the other what will nourish their perceptions, but that which will serve as background or as reserve to the dialogue must not prevent this from existing, must not paralyse it with a solitary welcome. Such a pause in the encounter has to remain a before or an after with respect to the moment in which each is venturing to open oneself to the other.

And if the risk is, in a way, lessened by what has already been perceived of the other, which allows us to run the risk again, it is also more difficult to take. It demands that we relinquish what we think we know about the other in order to enter anew into the night, without which the encounter will no longer take place, nor the rebirth of each one to whom he, or she, is.

Building the Between-Two

Remaining in the union from which our rebirth originates is, nevertheless, neither possible nor desirable. And freezing it within some institution or cultural prejudice makes it impractical, indeed non-existent. A pseudo-unity is then formed, a sort of conjoined production in which the alternation of being two and being one no longer exists. Such a going to and fro between the two and the one requires of us a relational cultivation – of looking, of listening, of all the perceptions, including touch, which is not exclusively reserved to the most intimate sphere of life, even if it permits us to reach it, provided that we pave the path.

Even embracing knows many degrees, stages, meanings – between the mother who hugs her baby to breast-feed, rock or pacify it; the father who clasps his son in his arms to pass on to him something of his strength or his clemency; a kiss between friends; all kinds of socially or politically coded embraces; the amorous embrace of lovers. Arms seem to make the same gesture; however, the difference is significant. It depends, in particular, on the degree of reciprocity between those who embrace one another.

If one is, somehow or other, higher up than the other, then it will be this one who embraces the other. Embracing can be a truly mutual gesture only between two persons extraneous to a hierarchical relation. And this gesture has seldom occurred given the traditional relation between man and woman. Perhaps it has more often existed between friends? But this meeting is not endowed with the same meaning. Embracing someone who is the same as oneself or different from oneself has a quite dissimilar effect on subjectivity. For the one who experienced the man–woman relationship only as a hierarchical relation – for example, between nature and culture, lover and loved one – the relationship between those who are the same can appear to be an amorous progress. For the one who did not yet feel what can occur through a non-hierarchical difference between the sexes, nor what it then opened as space between persons – given space and space yet to be built. Space which safeguards the transcendental dimension between the two without it being necessary or inevitable that this transcendence become set as an entity.

If such a space results from the restraint that the respect for the other as other requires of us, it must also become paths, passages, bridges between the one and the other. We have to make ways that allow us to go towards the other and also return to ourselves, to prepare journeys and places with the meeting in view, thus which preserve the singularity of each one and do not abolish the two in a fixed unity, a unity no longer alive but feigned, artificial. It is a matter of attaining a cultivation of the relation that escapes the imitation of the one, and of one's own necessities or ideals, by the other; which prevents a possible encounter; as is the case in a relation in which the one is the reflection or the image of the other. These reductions, which are in fact quantitative, of a difference and of a transcendence between the two mean that the other is constantly included in the one – or the One – and that the relations can only be conflictual and aggressive, the two not being able to love or desire one another.

There exist scenographies of possible enjoyment of the one by the other. Our tradition knows almost only these, but they amount to an exploitation of the one by the other and not to an encounter between the two, including through embracing. The texts of our culture regarding this are clear. What ought to be the most intimate union often ends in the triumph of predators towards a prey that they have succeeded in seducing. This masterful exultation is often followed by some sort of death or other, as is the case for certain animals that imprudently risk their sting or their venom.

There is nothing here like an approach to or in nearness – the lovers are more divided in, or after, making love than before embracing one another. Compelled by an attraction that is in some way blind, they begin to make love again, hoping that they will perhaps reach something else. All the efforts which are made to delude ourselves, either coming from the lovers themselves or from the environment, do not prevent the encounters, particularly the amorous encounters, in our culture from being seldom happy. It is so often the case that happiness, which ought to be our most precious objective, is considered by most adults as an adolescent dream.

It is true that desire and love demand a culture of the imagination, notably of the transcendental imagination, which our tradition has ignored. Hence the fact that relational life has become a source of disappointment, unhappiness, deterioration of the self, and not an opening of the horizon, a discovery of felicity, the blossoming of

oneself. Difference maintains the relation of the imagination to a transcendental dimension that always remains
beyond the reduction to an object or some entity. This
transcendental dimension is supported by the irreducibility
of the one to the other. The fact that desire longs for the
other, an other who cannot be reached, brings it back to
oneself, and preserves the opening to a beyond without
arresting it with some defined reality. The movement of
aiming at the beyond lasts because nothing anchors it in
a definitive way. Even though the impossibility of seizing
what attracts us outside our limits sometimes produces a
disappointment, it also ensures the revival of desire: its
indefinite appeal to an unattainable beyond for which it
continues to long.

Desire can be satisfied by progressing towards
transcending oneself, helped in this advance by love. Love
provides an equilibrium or a constancy that desire, which
always projects itself towards the beyond, neglects or
forgets, running, in this way, the risk of losing harmony, in
oneself and between the two.

What allows attraction to last is the preservation of the
duality in difference, and reciprocity in desire and love.
Such a reciprocity does not amount to giving back the
same but to bringing into play, on either side, an energy,
a movement, a warmth destined for the other. These
are inevitably different on the part of each one; which
guarantees the permanence of the transcendence between
the two.

In this sort of exchange, nothing is ever possessed, at
least in a definitive manner, without the bilateral participation being interrupted. What is felt, received as a surplus,

has to remain fluid, at the service of the becoming of each one and of the relation between the two. The same goes for well-being and happiness, which must be perceived as resulting from the two, and thus cannot be considered as personal property. Which, moreover, contributes to increasing them in an exponential manner.

Between the one and the other, a micro-culture is set up. It can become the leaven for a universal culture that keeps alive the energy of each one as well as that of the relation between the one and the other.

A living energy necessarily grows. If our cultures or societies become ossified, age, perish, it is because they are constructed from a fixed, one could say a dead, energy. The forms that structure them persist for a time, indeed proliferate like cancerous cells. However, life itself no longer ensures their development, that has become only quantitative and doomed to destruction by a shortage of living energy that ought to organize them, in themselves and between them.

To be sure, this energy needs limits. But instead of being imposed as definitive forms, even forms presumed to be ideal, these limits henceforth exist as the blossoming of the life of each one, that the relations with the other prevent from proliferating in anarchic, intrusive or despotic ways. The opening to the other, the encounter with him, or her, and the return to oneself continually produce moving boundaries – which provide a border for energy and allow it to blossom according to a living order. There are, thus, no longer limits imposed from an outside, formally abstracted from the present, but a being-in-relation that requires, at every moment, a restrained flowering for each one.

For such a flowering, letting be is as important as mastering. Our tradition has encouraged us to be effective, to make or fabricate but not to let be born or let be. A gesture which demands of us a relational economy, essential at the level of breathing, for example. In order not to freeze gestures and words, but also the longing or breathing, between us, it is necessary to intertwine intentional creation and letting be – in myself, in the other, between us. That to which our encounter gave birth cannot become an actualization on the part of each one alone. A letting be, and also letting oneself be, is, moreover, that which will indicate to me and to the other the impact of the event – or advent – that took place.

Such a letting be is what is most difficult for us. It forces us to relinquish the ideal of mastery that has been taught to us, not as an aptitude for staying within our limits in order to respect the other, but as an ability to dominate everything and everyone – including the world and the other – without letting them blossom according to what or who they are. Moved by nature, by the other, it will be difficult for us to leave them to their becoming until our next meeting. Now this can only happen if we run such a risk – letting go of any ascendancy over them, indeed any link with them, in particular with the other.

How to give again to the other the freedom to search for their own way when I have been made one with him, or her, when the other exists in myself, and I partly became the other? This task is in some way superhuman. Nevertheless, it is essential for the permanence of desire and love. Its difficulty is so great that we have invented a culture, indeed a God, in which we could become one. But this sealing of the between-two by a third party prevents us from meeting with one another – always joined, we have occupied the free space between us. As far as we are concerned, we only represent a part of a wider unity from which we barely emerge through a little differentiated attraction. We detach ourselves from the whole for just a moment, the time necessary for recomposing it, integrating ourselves within it even more firmly than in the past, contributing in this way to consolidating the cohesion of this whole. The family, for example, takes part in the cohesion of the State, and the traditional means of founding it clearly bears witness to such an objective. To call this traditional means into question, to deny it, no doubt ends in that destructuration of the family unit which we are today witnessing. Without changing our conception of desire and love, the family can be restored only from a moral foundation, even more rigid than in the past.

To consider a cultivation of desire as a new manner of establishing an amorous stability, possibly at the level of the family and community, requires reaching another stage of our human becoming – one in which the relations with the other as other are an essential dimension. Appropriation, property, possession, on which the family, indeed society, were based, must then be overcome thanks to a mutual respect between different subjectivities.

Traditional morality will be of little use to us here. It does not teach us how to let the other follow his or her own path, meet with whomever he or she desires, go where he or she wants. And a mere injunction, be it a personal one, will not be sufficient. Moreover, this will often be accompanied by doing as the other has done – for example, being unfaithful to one's partner – in order to save oneself from suffering, from bearing a blow or jealousy. Which could amount to adopting a nihilist amorous attitude in the name of a so-called respect for the freedom of the other or of oneself, or even to turning amorous relations into an egoistic hedonism that only aims for a momentary satisfaction, without taking care of the continuance of attraction, of love. Which does not solve any problem in relating to the other at a human level. The question, rather, is one of becoming able to turn a natural appeal, an affective or cultural affinity, into a relation in which longing for transcendence can transmute, transubstantiate affects. It is not a matter, for all that, of sharing a common transcendence but of elaborating the between-two as a site of cultivation of the transcendental reality born from the attraction in difference.

Attracted horizontally by the other, energy becomes a rising movement because of the impossibility of appropriating the other as such. In order to remain faithful to the carnal dimension of desire, energy, nevertheless, has to preserve a descending movement. My way of perceiving the other is consequently situated between the heavens and the earth, and the same would go for the other. Thus, no longer enclosed settings within which the one or the other would be kept captive but a sort of angle open onto a fluid perspective where the other moves, becomes, without me being able to fix, even to freeze, him, or her, within a horizon. Instead of projecting myself onto the other and imprisoning the other within my world, I recognize that the other has their own source and I perceive them with this source as background – the becoming of each one also being also entrusted.

Between the two is thus preserved a becoming that is still to be elaborated – for the one, for the other and for their relations. It is a sort of always virginal space safeguarded through the attention that each one accords to the other in their transcendent alterity.

The World of the Beyond

Coming into the World

Dwelling in the world cannot unfold with only oneself in mind: having oneself in mind must intertwine with having the other in mind, and even the relation between the two. Thus, the limit of one's own world does not really amount to a privation, but to an obligation to return to oneself in order to respect the other. This return to oneself is a faithfulness to one's self thanks to a faithfulness to the other, which builds, while deepening it, a world of one's own now limited in its extension. What lay beyond the projection of oneself and spread towards infinity becomes what can provide each world with borders and release possibilities of projects with the space-time of an encounter with the other in mind.

Trapped in a relational network – of objects, things, concepts, names … – the subject can now reopen the horizon and the weaving of relations without abruptly undoing it. It is no longer the concern about a unique being or existing, or a new project, that creates an opening, but the concern about another subject. One might also say: about another world.

Whoever lives in a world no longer has to project himself into the beyond in order to exist – ek-sist – with respect to a past and, in this way, provide himself with a future, that is, with time. He, or she, has to care about the existence of other worlds and, firstly, of another world: that of a subject different from himself. Such a gesture limits one's projection, compels each to a return, in a way to a withdrawal, which reopens the transcendence of the horizon, frees each from being rooted in a past that already included the future.

To come into the world is not only to find oneself alone on a deserted island. Of course, in a sense, this is the case: alone, we enter into life thanks to an autonomous breathing. This aspect of our existence is often forgotten. As is ignored what it would allow us to perceive of our entering into a weaving of relations that immerses us in another closure than the one known in the mother. To come into the world means to enter into an interlacing of relations between living beings, things, human subjects and other kingdoms – animal, plant, mineral – but also between human beings and autonomous organisms or objects of the environment fabricated by humans. This weaving is so complex that it is difficult to emerge from it. Moreover it exists before our coming into the world. Any new existence finds itself enveloped by a world – living or constructed – that pre-exists it and prevents human beings from perceiving the real by themselves and from making up their own mind and acting altogether freely. One who is born enters a world that predetermines their point of view, their choices, their present intentions or their future plans – inside a horizon that they believe they give in complete freedom to their world. In them, as subjects, and in such a horizon, the past, the present and the future mingle. But they cannot decide about that, at least not totally. Each individual of a historical era belongs, to a great extent, to the same world. What they consider to be their own – subjectivity, thoughts, feelings – is, in a way, common to a group, to a culture. Their most intimate beliefs or emotions are shared by many. And what they imagine to be their freedom is already conditioned by the relational weaving from which they thought it was distinguished.

In fact, totalitarianism imposes from on high a uniformity that in a certain sense already exists down below. The background of a sociocultural era determines the individuals in our cultures. This standardization from below is not as perceptible as the standardization overtly ordered by a dictator. But it exists and it manifests itself through many signs: the refusal of the foreigner is one such index, but so is the scholastic apprenticeship of compliance with cultural requirements; the compulsory submission to religious or civil norms that in a later epoch will be declared obsolete; the accepted ways of behaving, dressing oneself or speaking; the coded manners of entering into relations with the other.

In this basic standardization, this predetermined belonging to the same world, the relations themselves between individuals pre-exist the meeting between two particular individuals. They are inspired, dictated, ordered by norms, habits, styles that surreptitiously lay down the law, including in love and desire. To unilaterally blame this or that tradition is rather naive. To question the foundation of one's own tradition is more relevant, as well as more useful in preventing all standardization, here or elsewhere.

Two privileged dimensions allow us to open the structure of the world in which we are included from the very beginning: relations with nature as an autonomous living world and relations with the other.

Natural life has its own finality. Bending it too simply to his own project, man deprives himself of a fruitful opening for the elaboration of his world. Nature can serve as a spectacle to be contemplated, as food, as a space to meet the other outside of respective closures and isolations. Nature represents possible inter-worlds – it belongs to all living beings and to none. It ought to serve as a space of mediation between all, but that requires it to be subjected by, or to, none. Unfortunately this is not the case. Man ought to be the one who helps the life that surrounds him, putting at its service, and for his own advantage, his specific aptitudes. The plant world acts in this way, regenerating the air by metabolizing what has destroyed its properties. Man could act in this way towards nature: arranging spaces for its development, contributing to the fruitfulness of the earth, pruning the surplus branches of the tree or the shrub in order to favour their growth. Some epochs or some civilizations have understood their role towards nature in this way; others have behaved as exploiters or rulers of the life surrounding them. Which little by little, but implacably, has turned against humans and their own existence. The living environment is necessary to their survival, but also to their culture or cultivation, notably of the relation to themselves and to others.

Behaving like a master towards the nature that surrounds him, man has appropriated that which could be used as a space of meeting between all living beings, between all that exists. Exercising a domination over the environing world, man has been damaging life itself, including his own and that of the other. In fact, nature, as a space of life, must serve the becoming of each one as well as a coexistence in difference. Nature is a universal that is shareable by all, males and females, men and women, and can thus be of use in mediating between all. The same does not apply for already constructed worlds and cultures. They are neither universal nor easily shareable. And one of them cannot act as mediation between the others. Now each lives in a world, one's own world, and is most often unaware of the existence of different worlds, and of the fact that the other does not necessarily live in the same world as oneself. Each believes that the other belongs to the world into which one was born.

But if coexistence with other humans means sharing the same world, this coexistence is established by what already exists. The perception of the other, of the space and the interactions between myself and the other, are ruled over by a single reality worked out before a subject comes into it, and this reality is imagined to be the same for all. Coexisting then presupposes belonging to a same world that regulates relations with oneself, with the other, with the environment. Being with the other in that case precludes that this other belong to a different world, that he, or she, not share our own world.

Nevertheless, the essential task that we have to carry out in our times is: how to coexist in respect for difference(s)? To what common horizon could we bend the diversities that have appeared to us – between nations, traditions, cultures, but also between generations, between sexes?

How could we force all of them to share a unique world other than through a totalitarian construction worse than all those which we have already known? What world could organize the being-with of all these different subjectivities? By means of what embracing horizon? At the price of what abstraction from the real? Of what dehumanization?

One of the urgent questions posed by our times – dominated by technology, long-distance communication, international markets, globalization ... – is: how to reorganize being with the other? Because coexistence can no longer take place inside and through a single world. We do not all belong to the same world, unless we designate the earth itself in this way. But, even on this earth, we do not all live in the same way. Not only because we are rich or poor, live along the beach or in the mountains, are farmers or city dwellers, but because we relate differently to nature, and to the other: to ourselves as or in nature, to the other as or in nature. Such is the case for man and woman, who cannot share the same relation to the natural world, whatever the appearances may be.

As a result of woman including man in pregnancy and, already, in love itself, the relations between including and included are not the same for the two sexes. It is therefore only in outward appearance that they coexist on earth. This has been intuited by most traditions before being forgotten in a more undifferentiated construction of the world, which varies according to age, region, faithfulness or unfaithfulness to the real in cultural elaboration. Still today, and whatever the artificial nature of our civilization, it is obvious that men and women do not live in the same way being-within and being-with. How then to coexist if not through authoritarian structures unilaterally imposed on them which do not favour a sharing of the world? If the one envelops the other, how could they be with one another, whatever the possible reversals of this enveloping – notably between nature and culture, immediacy and construction, near and far, past and future?

Of course, man and woman seem to be in the same natural or constructed world. But the relational weaving into which they are situated is not the same. It could appear similar only from an external viewpoint or after the imposition of structures or norms to which the one, the other, the two must submit. In that case, the relation of the living subject to the world is interrupted – it is no longer in his or her own world that man or woman lives, but in a fabricated world where they are in exile, each one, and the one with respect to the other.

Sharing the world between man and woman, men and women, is quite complex. Such a difficulty explains why the structure that organizes societies and cultures largely amounts to rules of coexistence between the sexes, either at the level of marriage and alliance or at the level of genealogy. The passage from nature to culture between the sexes has, more or less blindly, determined all traditions. But this passage is not resolved for all that. It was probably necessary to reach an epoch in which subjectivity is further and more subtly considered so that the modalities that are imposed for the coexistence between man and woman, men and women, appear as a resort to a sort of violence that paralyses human becoming. Neither the institution of marriage as such, nor laws which intend to guarantee it, nor customs, nor the background of the conjugal or

69

family home – with what it presupposes as the acquisition or appropriation of property – nor even the procreation of children are sufficient to create a world common to man and woman. They do not live in the same world, even when dwelling in the same house, sleeping in the same bed, joining their bodies, indeed their souls, in love. The painful and insurmountable nature of their strangeness to one another often leads them to believe that turning back to a natural immediacy could restore them to a lost belonging to a same world.

No doubt, in love man and woman sometimes for a moment become just one, creating a common world built from the energy of their attraction to one another and from some conjunction of being-within and being-with, which most of the time does not exist and is experienced as lost due to nostalgia for a first relation to the mother. Their being-with and their being-within, for a moment, harmonize the one with the other, at a bodily and spiritual level. This does not last and is partly illusory. But, for a time, the exile of each one in a world in which the other cannot dwell seems to be overcome. For a time, the invisible covering that divides each one from the other seems to vanish. The one and the other seem to be returned to this natural site where they were in communion with one another through the same air, the same breath, the same energy, uniting them through a sharing of the surrounding world. At least this would be their quest, which they approach in a more or less ecstatic way. With difficulty combining instasy and ecstasy, the most elemental aspect of life and the most sublime dimension of desire.

This common world in which it happens that they dwell

for a moment is built by the two. It does not exist before its elaboration by the two, whether it be faithful to the real or illusory – faithfulness to the real being what permits a participation of the two in the construction of a shared world.

The Desire for the Beyond

The project to construct this common dwelling has its origin in an attraction or desire of the one for the other. No doubt, this attraction or desire in some way exists before the meeting: coming into the world means entering into a weaving of relations where attraction and desire are already present. The world in which each one was born is potentially opened by the desire for the other. It will really become open as soon as desire is cultivated between the two. Otherwise relational energy, which is at work in desire, is harnessed by all kinds of objects, things, images, words and concepts. That which was a possible opening of the horizon closes up again in a confusion of relations of which the subject is a prisoner more than a player. The other as other no longer takes place, nor does the surplus that this other represented with regard to the closure of the horizon.

The longing for the other calls for a beyond of a world of one's own. It is a longing for transcendence in relation to any exclusively personal plan or projection. In order that this longing not be disappointed in its transcendental quest, it is essential that a subject irreducible to all forms or modalities of one's own world correspond to it. It is necessary that the call meet with another freedom that can never be assimilated nor even situated in a single and same world. The two desires must be faithful to the one who awakened them, but on the condition they cultivate together the longing for transcendence that they arouse. This is a difficult quest! The only one, however, through which humanity really becomes accomplished as humanity. But the path is never paved once and for all, never predetermined. The path is to be cleared, explored, created by each one and together, with opening and faithfulness to oneself and to the other. No already defined transcendence can be unilaterally imposed on the one or on the other. This would amount to again closing the opening of the horizon carried out by the call for transcendence. Some figures will perhaps be able to serve as beacons if they do not paralyse the longing of the one or the other for a beyond, and do not screen them from the risk that the opening to the other represents as calling for a beyond. What matters is to free and cultivate energy, a relational human energy still and always to be discovered and elaborated – in oneself, for oneself, for and with the other.

This energy means that what was considered as facticity – for example the body of which Sartre spoke and of which most Western philosophers did not speak because of its presumed antagonism to spirit – is already animated by that which, from the very beginning, establishes human subjectivity: a relational weaving, uniting each existence with the whole of the world in which it is situated. The question concerning the becoming of humanity is about the degree of freedom that subjects could secure for themselves with respect to the confusion of networks in which they come into the world – networks which exist before them and that, in a certain sense, their existence tears open or, at least, partially opens from the moment they live in an autonomous way. Each one, nevertheless, is trapped in a multiplicity of relations and one's first opening to the world is, in part, an unrecognized apprehension of a confinement. This mood will be confirmed by a surrounding pressure, a culture, an education that constrains us to be in accordance with that which exists before us. It will be suggested that each must defer the longing for a beyond with regard to the world in which one dwells into the transcendence of another world, without intending to modify, in one's own name, the world of which one becomes a guest. When the culture of this world lacks transcendence, each one will instead be invited to invest his or her desires in competitiveness, conquest, appropriation, expansion or accumulation. The yearning for a beyond is thus badly directed, and the subject remains split between angel and animal, without an appropriate cultivation of their wish for a beyond with respect to this world.

Certainly some geniuses will succeed, through their creations, in channelling their longing while slightly transforming the world that existed before them. In fact, a more universal means exists for cultivating attraction towards the other; it requires a cultivation of desire, turning attraction into a specifically human mood.

To cultivate attraction requires it not being harnessed or paralysed by already defined habits, norms, surrounding objects, things, gestures and discourses. It requires keeping the impetus alive without submitting it to an impersonal or neutral environment, which intends to master it through laws. The awakening of energy has to remain vigilant and attentive to its source, without letting it be reduced to the anonymity of a 'there is' – an already existing desire that is to be lived in one way or another according to the advice of parents, teachers or public opinion. Attraction cannot be sacrificed to anyone or anything, including even the most sublime cultural constructions. It must first be brought back to the one who awakened it. Not, of course, through merging into this source. The falling off of desire, its decline, comes from a loss of all singularity in an undifferentiated 'someone' or 'there is' that is already there, but also or at the same time from merging with who or what awakened it – from becoming, in some way, the other. This lack of differentiation prevents the cultivation of attraction by annihilating what aroused it: the difference between two subjects.

Amazingly, desire disappears if we do not take care of it: instead of being inclined to maintain the difference that awakened it, it tends to abolish this difference by all possible means. At least, this is the case in our tradition. Desire would like to capture, to possess, to appropriate the other, especially in their nakedness, or it searches for similarity, sameness, identification with – all ways of reducing or annihilating difference. What makes desire a cause of decline is the lack of consideration for its original and singular nature, and for the intersubjective context in which it arises.

The fallen aspect of desire has unfortunately been endowed with a moral connotation instead of being interpreted as unfaithfulness to ourselves and to our becoming. From such a perspective, our moral and religious traditions have often encouraged us to neglect a cultivation of our desire, so that we have regressed to animal instinct while projecting ourselves towards or onto models of divinities that are strange or mute with respect to a possible fulfilment of desire, in ourselves and between us.

All this has left us at once serene, unconcerned and restless with regard to the uncultivated, inhuman, unhappy, and 'fallen' – as Heidegger said with a particular meaning – character of our intersubjective relations. Where we are called upon to accomplish humanity as such – each one in a unique and irreplaceable manner – we evade the task and dissipate the energy born from the attraction between us into a thousand and one more or less febrile activities, which allow us to forget our essential disquiet and unhappiness. The most important part of our culture is devoted to maintaining such a dissipation, oblivion, loss of ourselves and of the other in the facticity of an already existing environing world.

The other as such has not been sufficiently considered as an essential dimension of our belonging to the world – the other from whom we receive ourselves, the other towards whom we project ourselves, the other who modifies our ability to be. If our horizon is determined by an original ability to be, it is closed. It is open if we accept that this ability to be is not received once and for all but evolves according to our relations with the other, an other who both limits and increases our ability to be. The other limits it because I can no longer be the totality of the whole. The other enjoys an ability of Being different from mine, which he or she fertilizes through a perception of the world that is not mine, through the energy that he or she brings to my existence, and the obligation imposed on me to free myself from the influence of an already existing world, from the reduction to facticity. I thus receive an original possibility to be – notably from the one who brings me into the world – but this possibility to be evolves thanks to the other who coexists with me in the world. My becoming is not only established by an initial ability to be, it is also received from this non-Being or this different Being with regard to me: the other. What I can foresee of my own Being is thus partial. In the accomplishment of myself, a contribution from the other will play a part that I cannot completely anticipate, unless I nullify the existence of the other as other.

What was imagined as freedom by philosophy is thus to be rethought: the dimension of respect for the other as a subject who limits my freedom but restores my impetus by reopening my own world is not sufficiently envisioned. The Western philosopher considers that the relation to the world is determined by a single centre or source, a single opening to the world. Now the freedom of the other represents another opening, another project or centre with respect to the world. I have to take that into consideration in order to freely define my own project. This cannot amount to an infinite projection that includes the other as one being among others. In such a case, my freedom is in part imaginary or fictitious. My project must necessarily take into account that of the other, which stops its expansion towards the infinite and contrasts another transcendence with my own, notably the one that I am for the other. The same goes for my comprehension, which comes up against the irreducibility of the other to my understanding. Such limits to the expression of my ability to be force me to exist – or ek-sist – with respect to the world otherwise than through a project that exceeds or transcends the network of relations in which I am situated. It is no longer only by myself that I transcend my being already there through projecting myself into the beyond; rather it is through accepting to stop before the irreducibility of the other, a stop that makes me differently ek-static with regard to the world determined by me.

My existence – or ek-sisting – is also received from the other through a gesture where doing and letting do, being and letting be, activity and passivity intertwine. But such a passivity is in some way active, as it is respect, welcome, hospitality towards the Being of the other. It lets happen, in myself as well, this other towards whom my ability to be cannot be only activity or personal initiative. The sense of the other, that I have to consider for the accomplishment of myself, makes me enter into another world of meaning, in which the relational weaving is still to be elaborated.

If my desire is reduced to a sharing of what is already common, it loses its impetus: the energy that drives it on becomes frozen in what is already there. What allowed it to exist – to ek-sist – becomes a cause of its burial in facticity. And the more energy is invested, the more mobility, or life, becomes paralysed.

I must do my best not to affect in advance the Being of the other. This Being has an original situation in a proper world and exists through a proper project. The Being of the being that corresponds to the other is neither comprehensible as such by me, nor reducible to my own project. I have to preserve for the other and around him, or her, an opening to the world that is proper to them – this belongs to the sense of the other. I cannot approach the other only according to some viewpoint or other, some dimension or other, on pain of never meeting them as other. The other is a totality that I have to respect as such, without submitting them to my own perspective, unless I reduce them to merely being within the world – which a subject cannot be.

Objects, concepts, and sometimes things need my project to be endowed with a meaning. The same does not go for the other, who is by himself, or by herself, a source of meaning. The disclosure of the other as such can happen only thanks to a withdrawing of my project towards them, a withdrawing that lets the other appear as they are. The other cannot take place in my own world: the other only takes place beyond the horizon of my world. Wanting to meet the other inside my own horizon prevents the other from ever taking place as other – in front of me, for me, with me. My world cannot be the background from which the other appears to me: the other is then overshadowed by what I projected of myself onto them. Solicitude for the other thus partly amounts to suspending all projections or plans about them.

The Ecstasy of the Encounter

If the project of a woman is, first of all, relational and that of a man, first of all, solitary, how can they meet together? What present or presence are possible between them? Going to meet the other cannot submit to mere anticipation: another temporality has to be set up. From the perspective of a single subject, temporality is built between the past and the future, with a mutual involvement of the two. The present is the place where the past and the future are formed through their interaction. The present, in a way, is the bridge between the past and the future, the future and the past. If relating with the other is considered to be a decisive dimension in the accomplishment of each one, temporality proves to be more complex: the presence of the one to the other becomes the place where two temporalities are linked together. The future of each one is then modified, and thus the relations between past and future, from which the temporal bridge was built.

Death can no longer be what univocally determines my temporality. A cultivation of life, in which each one participates, leads us to another temporality in which the future will never be a simple achievement of my past. And in which the different phases of my temporality can no longer simply coexist.

Meeting the other acts as a tear in my temporal weaving, a tear which also corresponds to a necessary realization of latent dimensions of my existence and my Being. Nearness to the other in the present never amounts to nearness to myself. The present thus becomes dual: a present in which I return to myself, in myself, in order to gather with myself and gather all that by which I have been affected, and a present in which I make myself available for the other in the encounter. I will never succeed in rendering the other present to me all by myself: the other is not a being merely there, at my disposal, as a part of the world. To open myself to the other requires that I open myself to an other Being, who prevents my world from closing up in a totality that includes all beings. The one to whom I open myself in this way remains incomprehensible to me, and such an opening to the other also renders me incomprehensible to myself, although it is a disclosure of what or who I am. This disclosure is of a transcendental nature.

If the attraction that brings me towards the other is a quest for transcendence, as a desire for a beyond that I cannot appropriate in my world, and if the same goes for the other towards me, what calls us together belongs to a transcendental dimension. It is in a transcendental ecstasy that we exist together if what brought us closer is a relation of desire between us, and not a mere complicity within an environing world that is already there and supposedly the same for the two. If this were merely the case, what attracts us towards one another would already be a decline of desire, and not a respect for desire and its cultivation as an impetus that releases us from our submission to, or alienation in, the already there.

The other is, in their own way, a future that is present in the present without any past in this present. At least this is the case in the first meeting with the other, but it will always be partly so: the other cannot belong to my past. The other has to remain transcendent with respect to my own temporality. The memory of the other must maintain a possible outside or beyond in relation to any appropriation. The other invites me to a dis-appropriation that is also a dis-alienation of my adherence to, or confusion with, a world that is already there. The other carries me away from the facticity of my past, while committing me to a transcendental faithfulness to this past.

The other forces me out of facticity, at least in the moment of our meeting, if I open myself to the transcendence that he or she is for me. I will have to be faithful to the ecstatic character of the moment of encounter without the whole unfolding of my temporality becoming suspended there. The work of Being and becoming what or who I am compels me to a return to myself. But all that will from then on appear to me will lose the immediacy into which I merged. To be faithful to the meeting with the other as an essential dimension for my life opens a real perspective to me with regard to the perception of what I approach in the present. This distance from immediacy gives another weight to all that presents itself to me, and interrupts the inexhaustible stream of things upon which my adhesion confers a general equivalence.

The comprehension of objects or things of the world is reorganized starting from the comprehension offered to the other, an a priori comprehension, such a free space-time in which it will be possible for the other to appear without ever being understood. The comprehension of every being is modified according to the sort of comprehension that I must show in co-existing with the other as a subject dwelling in a world different from mine. Henceforth I have to dwell in my world without simply merging with it, independently even of a proper project that goes to the limits of my Being. In fact, the opening to the other as other imposes on me limits that suffice for removing me from the facticity of my already being there. This opening makes relative the absoluteness of my environment and of my project with a view towards co-existing with another subject in respect for our difference(s). I must not forget the already-there that constitutes me, but neither must I forget the ecstasy of a being-with-the-other, faithful to the moment of our coming, the one and the other, into presence. I have to take care of these two dimensions that are essential to the constitution of my temporality: remembering myself and remembering the other, caring about the two while letting them be in their difference(s). Which requires me not to hold the other through an appropriation that makes me unfaithful to each of us.

The other cannot be destined to the one, reduced to an instrument of one's own ability to be or one's own achievement. A subject cannot be confused with a tool at the disposal of one who would like to use it. Unfortunately this has often been the case in the attraction between man and woman. A lack of cultivating desire has resulted in one – most often the man in our tradition – making use of the other in order to fulfil one's own plan. This has generally happened in sexual, but also procreative, relations. Woman has become nature-earth-matter at the disposal of an activity of man. There is nothing there that is specifically human. If a purpose exists between subjects, it ought to be a reciprocal purpose between the one and the other. Sexual difference corresponds to such a purpose so long as we do not go back to equipmentality, to using the other as a piece of equipment, or to an instinct that forgets the singularity of the other's world. To be destined-to then necessarily means that one world calls on the other world in order to humanly achieve one's own Being, but also that of the other, that is to say, to achieve humanity as such.

For this to happen, the two must be maintained. Thus the one cannot appropriate the other, keep the other as a part of one's self or possess the other as an object or a thing of one's own world; and the other cannot give their self up to the one, forget their self in the one – nor even in the One – relinquishing the fulfilment of their own destiny. If the one and the other are not safeguarded in their difference(s), desire between them vanishes. The one is not satisfied with an object that no longer arouses attraction: like a tool that has become unusable; and the other no longer feels desire for the one with or in whom he, or she, merges.

The decline of desire is due to its reduction to need, to the subjection of its impetus to a 'for what?' and not 'for whom?' it was destined. In this forgetting of the other as such, the subjectivity of each one has been used to motivate the inadequate nature of the relation. But instead of this relation becoming intersubjective, the disappointment of the attraction-for turns into rejection or exclusion, and a return of each one to a solitary project.

The fact that the other cannot remain a permanent pole of attraction has not yet led us to cultivate our relations in such a way that no one is reduced to a thing useful to the other. The ecstasy, the one with regard to the other, of the worlds of the two subjects has not been preserved, and their meeting has thus become impossible. The ecstatic dimension of the situation has been appropriated by at least one of the subjects in his, or her, temporal relation to the world, with the other having fallen into this. What each blindly rejects is the non-presence of the other to oneself as a subject. Each rejects what is not appropriate to one's own desire: that which is unable to support our ecstasy against a submission to a world already there, wrongly confused with our earthly existence.

All the strategies about lack – of the other or in the other – that aim to revive attraction are deceptions showing how much humanity is unfaithful to its destiny. The 'lack of' put forward as a means for arousing desire is at best like the red cape that is waved to urge on the fighting bull. Except that the red cape is there whereas the 'lack of' means an absence in relation to the representation that we imagine of the other as other. This absence will never be similar to the red cape of the bullfighter; our attraction does not for all that have to project itself into emptiness but instead turn itself towards one who is able to support its ecstasy. It is not henceforth a 'lack of' that attracts us, but the fact that another subject remains beyond all the objects of the world that we can think. The other provides for their own appearing starting from a freedom that is their own, from a world and a project that are their own.

'To be destined to' can mean something quite different from 'being of use to', at least in a certain sense. 'To be destined to' in the relation between man and woman ought to evoke what cannot 'be of use to' because it does not belong to the same world. Certainly, we could say: it is of use to maintain an attraction towards the beyond, to keep aiming at some transcendence. But is it then fitting to speak of 'to be of use'? Unless we understand this in an almost reverse sense: the other is useful as long as he or she cannot be of use, that is, as long as they escape their reduction to a tool. Unfortunately this has seldom been thought about in this way between the sexes. Sexual difference has instead been reduced to an implement, considered in terms of possessing or not possessing the adequate instrument in order to make love or procreate. The one who did not have the necessary tool was supposed to provide for matter and place at the disposal of the tool.

The human dimension of the difference between man and woman requires us to overcome this instrumental horizon. This requirement has often been confused with a sexual abstinence instead of encouraging us to cultivate the relations, including the carnal relations, between subjects who are different. This cultivation demands of us a new way of relating to the present – the present will no longer remain only a bridge between past and future, future and past. The present now corresponds to the time of an ecstasy in which opening to another world becomes possible. The temporal ecstasy of the present is thus articulated with a spatial ecstasy. But the two are just as well enstases because the attraction for the other and the desire for the beyond already take place in myself.

An additional opening becomes what returns us to ourselves, within ourselves, more than a simple temporalization could have done. Furthermore, if my understanding of the other as such amounts to arranging a space in which the other can appear, it is now he, or she, who will secure their own presentation. This allows me to remain in myself without having to divide myself for such a gesture. The other stops my projection towards the infinite. The other intervenes in my project, of which they increase or correct the ecstasy towards a beyond that was only mine. The other arrests my impetus towards a future, to which only death gave a horizon, by setting against it the limit imposed by another transcendence, that of the other. Such a transcendence has a share in life itself but it is even more irreducible than the transcendence of death, which does not prevent my imagination from making up worlds that do not exist.

The other exists before me not to send me back to my own temporality through their absence – as Lévinas affirmed in an explicit way and Heidegger in an implicit way – but to hinder it and call for another elaboration of temporality: for a being with the other that lasts. Which disconcerts our logic. No syllogism that sustains our truth foresaw an economy of being with the other as other, not even the logical sequence tied to instrumentality: if ... then. In fact, another logic is to be invented.

The Transcendental Truth of the Other

The other does not, in fact, belong to my world. As in a scientific approach, we have to isolate the other from the environing world in order to allow the other to appear. It is beyond the references belonging to our relational world that the other can appear to us, without the objectivity in question being the same as in the exact sciences, however. The other is irreducible to any object, pre-given or constructed by our plan. The other does not for all that lack objectivity, but this is in great part determined by their own subjectivity. Of course, the other has a bodily reality that can be approached scientifically. And the same goes for their psychic existence. But the centre from which the other organizes the whole of himself, or herself, cannot be conceived of like an object of science. It is possible to come near to it through the analysis of discourses, of gestures or works produced. But this organizing hearth evolves, and what can be understood of it must contribute to the arrangement of a space of freedom around the other, rather than to their imprisonment within patterns that paralyse their mobility and their becoming.

Compelling me to an opening in time, the other also compels me to an opening in space. The other asks me to interrupt the composition of my own weaving of time and space, not in order to go from a subjective to an objective perspective – as is the case in a scientific approach – but to be capable of meeting another subjectivity. This requires me to reorganize the relations between time and space, but also between subjectivity and objectivity. The objectivity of the other cannot be reduced to any object; it corresponds to a reality irreducible to any subjectivity, but is, however, a perceptible expression of it, a sort of phenomenal projection of the existence of the other. The singular nature of such an objectivity lies in the fact that the reality of the other is both natural and constructed. The objectivity of the other's presence is in part structured as the reality of a living being, but also as the result of the impact of an external action on this living being. This intervention comes from the world, from objects or things, from the other(s), but also from the effect of one's own actions on each one.

The transcendence of the other with regard to me is simultaneously that of the plant, in part that of an animal but also that of a human being. It is complex and asks me to stop my journey in order to let the other be and also to let happen to me, within me, what the presence of the other may provoke.

No scientific method can take into account the other as such: the other is irreducible to any object, be it natural or constructed. And no pre-established pattern can allow their presentation as other. It is only by himself, or herself, that the other – if they exist – can appear in a manner that is each time new and unpredictable, depending on the space and time. The sole a priori starting from which I can approach the other is respect, that is, a going-towards that will as well be a withdrawing-before and -around the other in order to let this other exist and be. This will also allow me to consider the other outside the relational network that composes my own world. Here again there is no question of the other being reduced exclusively to an appearing, even if this is decisive in the relation to him, or her. If relating to the other precludes the other being at my disposal as tool, as matter or as space-time with a view to elaborating my own world, I cannot confine myself, with regard to the other, to the perception of an appearance. No doubt this appearing is critical at the level of truth – mine, that of the other, that of the world – but appearance does not for all that correspond to all the elements that enter into my relationship to the other. And we lack words to refer to the acts that unite us, in which the various dimensions of ourselves take part.

Truth is involved in this being in relation – truth of each one, truth in the relation to the world as well as to the history of humanity, truth in the relation itself. In our tradition, however, truth has too often been considered to be something exclusively mental, unless it has been treated as the reality of natural beings, of objects or things of the world. The link between natural and affective or spiritual existence has remained almost unthought. Truth and love have most of the time been viewed as barely compatible, indeed antagonistic; and the same has happened with love and life. In the encounter with the other, these dimensions intervene in a different way from the one at work in the relations of a solitary subject with the environing world. This way of relating – pre-given, pre-established, indeed even imposed upon us – from which I can emerge only through my existential project, is put into perspective and made relative by what the encounter with the other asks of me, notably in order to constitute my subjective wholeness.

The respect for the other as other interrupts my dependence on the world because it compels me to open to another transcendence. This availability towards the transcendental dimension opened by the other undoes the weaving of the relations that structured the world for me, especially their bonds of subordination. For a moment, the totality of the world is kept in suspense to welcome the other, a stranger with respect to my world. To this world I will never return unchanged: I will have gained a new freedom but lost the familiarity that I maintained with my own environment. Through the meeting with the other, what seemed to me close has become partly strange because I distanced myself from my world in order to open myself to the world of the other.

If our tradition has believed that the relation to the other is determined and made possible by sharing the same world, henceforth we know that it does not depend simply on this. Even if we the one and the other exist at the same time in the history of humanity, we do not necessarily belong to the same historical configuration if we are not situated in the same culture.

But other differences have begun to appear between us that make relative what is common in belonging to the same time in history. Perhaps some of us are then living in the same construction of the world. But the objectivity of what surrounds us is not, or ought not to be, the whole of our subjectivity; otherwise the encounter with the other as other would be impossible. It can take place only outside, on this side or beyond, a predetermined objectivity. The fact that we were born at the same time, indeed in the same place and in the same culture does not suffice to allow us to enter into relation with one another. We may then share some properties, but this does not yet mean to communicate between us as different subjects. This sharing, which in a way is imposed on us, could even prevent an exchange between us. It makes us parties to a world that is already there, and thus contributes towards again closing its horizon. This deprives each of us of the transcendental dimension necessary for our human becoming and the relation between us.

Transcendence was often brought to us by the world itself, either as an entity already defined in its horizon – God or the Truth, for example – or through the formation of the totality of a world. In both cases, transcendence was useful for constituting our subjective unity. We have not thought enough about the fact that, from the very beginning, we had to deal with a double, indeed a triple, unity. The perception of our environment as a horizon amounts to one unity: this is generally designated as a world. In our coming into the world, the other provides for another source of the gathering of our self. The other does not correspond to some object in the world, and he himself, or she herself, appears as a totality towards whom we have to situate ourselves. But how can I do this with regard to the first one who surrounded me, and has been the first world in which I took place: my mother? I initially reached my own unity, with respect to her, through breathing by myself.

Relational life thus gets organized, from the very beginning, between three totalities: that of the environing world, that of the other, and my own. None of these can be sacrificed to the other without the connection with transcendence becoming ruined. I cannot merely provide myself with it, but nor can it be imposed on me simply by the other. A dialectical process must be established between my existential plan and the reality of the other. My will to be must allow limits to its expansion. It must accept the stopping of an infinite projection: the opening to the other.

It belongs to the achievement of a human being to want to not want on the other's behalf – to let his or her being be as different. We thus need to come to terms with two aims: that of our wish to extend endlessly while remaining in our own world and that of wanting the infinite in relating to the other.

This twofold aim corresponds to a double relation to transcendence. If the first of them has been envisaged in various ways in our tradition, the second has been neglected or deferred into the beyond of our world. The transcendence of the other, here present beside me, has become ecstatic through merging into the transcendence of the Other, the absolutely same, which remains an ideal inaccessible to me. This Absolute reinforces my projection towards infinity as the horizon of a world of my own, providing it with an additional space and time. It is no longer only my death that limits my projecting: an ideal of Being extends beyond my status as a mere living being.

Such a relation to transcendence – as a project extending to the horizon of one world or an extrapolation into a beyond determining the real of this world – does not allow me to accomplish my humanity. The relation to the other, essential for my own human achievement, is not yet approached in an appropriate way.

Our being in the world is relational. But the privileged relation is, or ought to be, the relation to and with another human. We probably expect to hear: with other humans. But to consider them straightaway in their multiplicity evades what relating to the other as a human being signifies. Taken as a whole, human beings form a single body with all the beings that form a world. The encounter between two subjects, which represents what is most specific to humanity, is not yet approached. If we are already in a certain mood, it is not yet towards this one, him or her, with whom we meet. Their singularity is still unfamiliar to us. In fact, our attitude has to be a welcoming mood, an opening to what stays beyond the horizon of our world. Trusting to a wisdom of our heart, to an awakening of an attraction, we accept in our nearness what remains incomprehensible to our mind, still unknown and not representable. We listen to a part of ourselves generally excluded from the field of reason, indeed of common sense. Running the risk of exposing ourselves to an unforeseeable becoming, a new growth. Putting our transcendence itself to the test of what has not yet happened. Recognizing that in the present, in the meeting with the other, we are not yet those who we really are, or ought to be. Our present has been a bridge between the past and the future, the future and the past, and not yet a space-time, a space in time in which the other appears to us – an event that probably corresponds to our desire but also questions the foundation of our subjectivity, undermining our world, moving the walls of our dwelling.

We are not yet what or who we ought to be in the approach between the other and ourselves. But our project alone will not allow us to reach that point – it jumps over the space of the entry into presence of the one and the other. It goes beyond without considering this beyond that the presence of the other is to me, without welcoming the future that will happen to me from the encounter with this other. A future irreducible to the mere unfolding of my past: the contribution of the other will enter into it.

I will have had to arrange for the coming of the other, to prepare a space in time in which the other can appear to me, in which I consent to receive and welcome him or her; but I cannot foresee, for all that, how the other will modify my existence – my already-have-been and thus my future – the development of my life. This will depend on the embodiment that will follow our meeting, on the engendering of the one by the other that will result from the encounter between our two singularities: of their welcoming each other, their fertilization of one another. This will depend on a hospitality offered to the other, including in myself, a hospitality that is without pre-established dwelling: entrusted to a letting be.

To become what or who I am will remain the task, but 'to what' I am destined henceforth intertwines with a 'to whom', without the one ever being likely to dissociate itself from the other. These two faithfulnesses have to guide my journey, my becoming. And my destination to be or to become a human being is what can adjust their interweaving.

Such an interweaving is, among others, an interlacing of space and time. A solitary project, a solitary relation to time does not suffice to allow a real subject to exist – or ek-sist. This mere temporal structuring cannot give an account of all transcendence of which a human being is capable. It transforms an already-being-in-the-world into a not-yet-being-in-the-world through an ecstasy of the present. But this link between space and time does not permit us to live, neither the one nor the other. Temporality is instead used by the subject to emerge from an already-being-in-the-world in order to give oneself a world of one's own. The relation to time goes from a utilitarian dimension to a transcendental dimension without a real change resulting from this passage. The space in which I was always already situated becomes the space in which I will never situate myself – always future with respect to the present in which I am.

I am never situated only by myself in the present human space and time. The other can call me back there, the meeting with a different subject. The crossroads between our two existences brings each of us back to ourselves. It calls us back to a dimension of ourselves that we had forgotten – a real, an opening, a transcendence that we had 'jumped over' in our becoming. It calls us back to a being-in-the-world decisive for us as humans, but which we had neglected: to be with the other as other.

This calling back to ourselves is also a calling back to the present. It is in the present that we can meet the other as such – a present that is no longer a mere bridge between having-already-been and having-yet-to-be. A present in which I am, I have to be, in order to meet with the Being of the other – the most constitutive meeting for the unity of my Being, but also the most risky, the most hazardous.

In such an encounter, all is, in a way, taken-away-from and given-back-to, but all is from then on different from the already-there in which I came into the world. That which has always been familiar and close is put at a distance because of the nearness prepared to welcome the other. The approach, indeed a partial intersection, between our two worlds modifies my way of perceiving my environment, making it more vague. Even my look is questioned by the perspective that the other compels me to have on my own world. Unless I merely integrate the other into it. But, then, the other no longer exists as other. At best, there remains a category of otherness through which I define, in which I enclose, the other in order to maintain the borders of my own horizon, instead of opening this horizon to the other world that the other is for me. Then I am put at a distance, sent to an ecstatic position regarding my already-having-been, including my relations to and with my surroundings, while I am brought back to a part of myself who was awaiting its advent – an advent related to the event of the encounter.

Distance in Nearness

The Home of Self-Affection

The other interrupts the system of cross-references of my world, re-opens my horizon and questions its finality. As such, the other undoes the familiarity that was mine. The other is always a stranger who crosses the limits of my territory and upsets my habits. My first gesture will thus be a gesture of refusal, of rejection, at best of integration or assimilation. In any case, the otherness of the other, the difference between us, is abolished.

Nevertheless, an appeal to the other exists in me. Something or someone, in me, is attracted towards this stranger to me. Something, or someone, who takes place in the most intimate core of my being – perhaps more familiar to me than the familiarity that I feel towards my own world. There is, in me, someone who is longing for the other as a condition for the appropriation of a familiarity more familiar than that of the world already known, as a condition for discovering an intimacy that I have not yet experienced. Such a wish for the other, for the coming of the other and the meeting with the other inside the horizon of my world, inside my most personal and inner boundaries, could be called: desire. No world, whatever its accomplishment and future might be, ought to reduce or kill this desire for the other. But desire is not fulfilled without hardships. And in order to evade the task that taking care of desire assigns to us, we often stop at nothing, including the sacrifice of humanity as such.

Desire compels us to progress in the becoming of our humanity. It asks us to overcome all dichotomies: body/ spirit, outward movement/inward movement, substance/ becoming, unity/duality, etc. A cultivation of desire needs us to be capable of questioning our world without, for all that, leaving it. Appealing to a relation still to be built, it demands that we be able to suspend the relational world that was ours – to open this world to the call of another world. Which does not mean to relinquish, to renounce our own world, but to bring it back to a possible becoming thanks to a relation for which I long but which will always escape the familiarity that I felt in a world closed only on, or by, my own subjectivity, whatever the relations taking part in it. Entering into relation with the other inside my own subjective horizon does not run the risk of calling this horizon into question for a becoming with the other, and the elaboration of a world that will be built by the one and the other without ever belonging to the one or the other.

The other stands in a space that I will never occupy. Through this, he or she eludes my relation to spatiality. What was familiar to me in the perception of space is disconcerted by the presence of the other. Unless I include this other within my world, which annuls them as other. Moreover, the other moves in space, and this prevents me from assigning to him, or her, a place where they would in some way be at my disposal. One of the meanings of the confinement of woman in the house is no doubt to keep her at the disposal of man in a fixed space. But the temptation of assigning to the other a space in order to keep them available for one's own project is rather common.

The fact that the other stands in a space inaccessible to me and that the other does not stay in a place fixed by me, or at least for me, means that nearness here is also always remoteness. Even when sitting at my side or present in front of me, the other remains distant, strange to me – the other does not dwell in my world.

The privilege of the same with respect to the other, the fact that most of the time the other is considered as an other-same or an other-of-the-same can be explained by the difficulty of calling into question the familiarity of the space in which I dwell. If the other is situated in the same world as me, or if I can imagine the world where the other dwells, this other no longer upsets the familiarity that I experience towards my surrounding space. Then the *epoché* of the perception of space – but also of the imagination – that the other imposes on me as other becomes groundless. Which suspends the transcendental dimension needed in the meeting with the other – including at the level of imagination. An imagination that then remains silent, it is true, but which restores a virgin space, still devoid of familiarity, and even of orientation, other than an availability to the other as other. And moreover to me, as a being beyond an undifferentiated but oriented world. One could speak here of a transcendental freedom, or of a freedom in relation to transcendence.

This freedom is mine. And although the respect for the other as other gives it back to me or allows me to accede to it, this freedom is not shareable as such. At least not directly. It is even the renunciation of an immediate sharing that permits me to discover and safeguard it.

In the space thus opened, or uncovered, the distance from the other cannot be overcome. I cannot bring the other close to me – the distance between us is insurmountable. I can get closer to the other, long for their transcendence, if this is safeguarded and kept, without ever being able to appropriate it.

The relation to the other as other opens and animates a place different from the space to which the familiarity within a single world had accustomed me. Such a place is uncovered only if I am capable of going beyond belonging to a single world without, for all that, cutting myself off from myself, from my culture, from my own world. I enter another space in which the field of attraction and orientation no longer obeys a single focus. I am no longer, in some way, the centre of the world or the centre of a unique world, even if this world has been inhabited before me. Desire attracts me to the other and tries to attract the other towards me. I am no longer the only one who has to aim to reduce the distance between us. This decision is incumbent on two wills, two desires, two intentions. Which makes the field of attractions and orientations complex. Which also makes it irreducible if each one maintains one's desire as one's own with respect to a different desire. If each one cultivates one's self-affection, a self-affection in which an attraction for the other takes a part that will be a source of emotion but also of movement on the condition that one also dwells in oneself.

This requires that we not be affected by the world in which we live without any possibility of turning back to ourselves – that is, of being in touch with ourselves through self-affection. It is not only by that which surrounds us that we have to be touched. Or, at least, such an affect must be accompanied by self-affection, which puts it into perspective. Even if the world, the other or others can question this self-affection, they cannot, for all that, substitute themselves for it. Now it is this that our culture commonly suggests to us as an economy of affect, indeed as an ethical model. Which makes intersubjectivity impossible, except as a co-belonging to the same world and not as a relating between subjects. Such relating demands that the way in which the other affects me should not be confused with my own self-affection, on pain of reducing this other to an instrument or an object for self-affecting. Which most often occurs, and thus prevents a relation between two subjects.

Such a self-affection is still to be discovered and cultivated by each one. It has to confront specific obstacles on the part of man and of woman. The still unresolved difficulty for the masculine subject is to leave the surroundings that he has given to himself as a substitute for the maternal world. The masculine subject makes use of the world in which he dwells for self-affecting more than the feminine subject does. This world is no doubt substituted for his first placental dwelling, whose role in his initial affects he has barely considered, no more than he has considered the role of the mother as first human relation, particularly with regard to sexual difference. Another motive explaining masculine behaviour is that the male sex is in some way outside of his body and internal self-affection thus cannot exist for the masculine subject, as is possible for a woman thanks to the self-touching of her lips. The ways of being in the world are thus rather different for man and woman.

The dependence of the masculine subject on the surrounding world in order to define his 'here' comes, at least in part, from his dependence on the maternal world, a dependence of which he has not yet become aware, has not yet explored, nor whose impact on the constitution of his own horizon has he assessed. What he experiences as his own centring, as familiarity and proximity, is, in fact, determined by a lack of differentiation with regard to the maternal world, which, historically, has been transformed into a gathering of 'one(s)' or a collective neutral 'one'. This sort of 'one' – as linguistics teaches us – amounts to an 'I' to whom is added a 'you', a 'he', a 'she' or a 'they'; that is to say, that this 'one' amounts to a 'we' in which persons are barely differentiated. Here it is a question of a 'we' – a masculine subject and a feminine world – in which partici-pants are hardly separated, thus a 'we' remaining at the stage of the 'one'. Into this 'one' are introduced, second-arily, the barely differentiated units of a group, whose members imagine they make up a number between them without seeing in what space they take place.

In order to again find his self-affection, the masculine subject thus has to free himself from a double lack of differentiation that prevents him from being autonomous: a lack of differentiation with respect to the world that, in the present, surrounds him but is already substituted for another world of which he has not become aware nor taken the measure: the maternal world.

For lack of going through such a stage, the masculine subject is in a way situated outside himself. He is in exile from his relational being, and what he feels as familiar and near remains strange to him. He does not perceive this, being unable to skim over a world that is not his own, a world in which he confines himself to what is useful, to foresight, a world in which he does not know desire except as fate, decay, unhappiness. The relation that the masculine subject has with the world prevents him from meeting with the other and discovering ties of familiarity and nearness with this other. An economy of the relation between two is impossible as long as the masculine subject has not gained an autonomy, a capacity of being in oneself, a dwelling in oneself and returning to oneself not ordered by dependence on an already existing world, wrongly imagined as his own.

The feminine subject no doubt enjoys an easier relation to self-affection because of her morphology – notably her sexual morphology – and thus the way in which relations with the other are determined. The morphology of her sex allows woman to touch herself, in herself, independently of any tool foreign to her sex, independently of any exteriority. Pregnancy is also accompanied by an internal process of self-affection. Nevertheless this privilege is not without risk: even in such a process of self-affection, the other can intervene. The other then separates woman from the self-affection that her morphology brings to her – already in herself, but also in love and motherhood, provided she does not project onto the other or leave to the other such a self-affection. Which can be brought about or encouraged by the fact that the masculine subject does not recognize this feminine ability, unfamiliar to his world.

Most of the time, the masculine subject blindly uses the feminine, confused with the maternal, both to constitute a world for himself and to self-affect himself immediately. He does not preserve for the feminine subject – whose autonomous existence he does not know or recognize – an internal and external world of her own. He intervenes in the feminine subject's process of self-affection without even being aware of his breaking in, which, moreover, he thinks necessary in order to leave his world and enter into the world of the other.

Preserving her self-affection is not easy for a feminine subject. Without recognizing the other as other, without arranging a space around this other that maintains the difference between the two and allows each to return to and within oneself, woman will find it difficult to protect her self-affection – this being continually merged with the need that the man has of her for his self-affection.

The space arranged around the other cannot be the result of a mere foresight with respect to this other, at least not of a foresight about anything that I could imagine starting from my own world. If it is a question of foresight, this cannot concern a need that the other would, in my opinion, experience. It can only be a matter of caring about the preservation of Being as such – that of the other and mine, mine through preserving that of the other.

Such a care requires a letting go of foresight itself. In the foreseeing that I practise within my own world, the other has no place for Being. The world of the other takes place outside mine, except as a possibility, an opening maintained in my horizon. It is through this opening that the other can appear to me, thanks to my relinquishing a purpose and a foresight that would only be mine. The other will not appear, for all that, as a merely subsisting being. The resistance the other sets against the surroundings that are familiar to me is not that of a thing. And when I will have divested this other of all the surroundings in which I had wrapped him, or her, the other will not be unveiled as a mere facticity. On the contrary, it is from this moment on that the other might begin to appear to me with surroundings that are their own – be they those of life itself or their own life, and also of the relational world that is proper to them. From the moment when I am able to leave behind my usual concerns and worries, free the space from the relational networks that have woven it, a place exists where the other may appear. Such an appearing of the other means having access to another way of looking at, another way of perceiving the world. It signifies the entry into a world I did not know and that, nevertheless, is mine – but not yet discovered.

Exiled in an Any One

This entry into a new world is possible because being with, or to, the other is always already constitutive of our existence and our way of being in the world. The first world with which the subject has to deal is the other. The first world of the subject is an other. Whether it is still in her body or born but dependent upon her, the little human lives in a world that is the world of its mother. Only little by little does it awaken to another world, initially thanks to its own perceptions. But this awakening is still widely reliant upon her: who offers to the child things to see, to listen to, to smell, to taste, to touch.

We do not yet know how the infant distinguishes what belongs to the mother from what belongs to an objective world of which she is, in some way, the mediator. We have imagined that the father was the one who introduces the child to objectivity. But this objectivity, in fact, already exists for the foetus. The foetus perceives objective things – certainly at the proprioceptive level, but also at the auditory level, to evoke only two types of perceptions that are already known from experiment.

The objectivity of the world that is mediated by the mother has been neglected, indeed forgotten, in what we consider to be our way of being in the world. Now it has been, it continues to be present in the subject. The subject is always already situated in a relational context in which an environment, including an objective environment, takes place. The unveiling of this relational context is decisive for becoming aware of an objective being in the world in which the other has taken part without this participation later being recognized.

When we argue about our being in the world, we generally forget this first environment of the subject. It is the case for Heidegger himself. He places the being-there of each subject in a relation of coexistence which implies that all subjects are, the one with respect to the other, in some way equal as being-there – that is, the other could be co-present with me in a world that is also mine. The other would thus dwell, at least initially, in the same world as mine, a unique world, in which I could meet him, or her. If the other is not then reducible to a thing, just as he or she is not reducible to a mere substance or availability, something of these dimensions remains through the fact that the other is supposed to live in the same world as me. The other is in a way the same as me, and is also here with me. The others would not be, for the philosopher, those who I am not, but only those among whom I too am. Our world would be common: we would coexist in the same surroundings.

Such an opinion, which would like to be without any a priori, in particular any theoretical a priori, forgets that the other, like myself, has belonged to a maternal world proper to each of us. To assert that we are with one another in the same way and that the world is common to us amounts to cancelling this first existence that we have lived and that makes up part of our manner of perceiving the world and of situating ourselves in it.

Even the dimensions of the 'here' and 'there' are determined by this first relation. How can I call to myself this one who, at first, has surrounded me? How can I simply place outside myself this one who has provided me with the air and, later, the milk necessary for my life? How can I affirm that I am in the world with my mother, in a common world that we share? How can I claim that I am in the world as a girl in the same way as a boy, given that I place myself in relation to the first other, my mother, in a different way? And what, in this case, do the words: 'the same as', 'with' and 'common' mean? Do they not indicate a lack of consideration for my own existence and for the experience that I have of the world, an experience in which the relation with the other precedes what has been lived of the surroundings apparently shareable by all, men and women?

Of course, we meet one another starting from our belonging to a world, but this world is not the same, notably because the economy of our original relation with the mother, the first other, is not the same. If the masculine subject still and always places himself as 'here' starting from some 'there', it is precisely because in this 'there' a presence of the mother as first environment intervenes, which is unrecognized as such. What the masculine subject first searches for in his concern towards the world is the original care of his mother, a care reversed into his concernful activity – an activity that is not really free and autonomous because it depends upon a 'there' always already imposed as a world. Not only as an accumulation of subsisting things, but also as the place and horizon in which they are linked together. The concern that the subject has for the world is also a nostalgia for her original care for him, which he cannot leave behind because he has not been concerned with it.

Thus in his manner of dwelling he confuses the 'here' where he ought to be with the 'there' which would be the place of her for him. The 'there' of her has entered into him, where he tries to contain it with a house of language, a weaving of words that link him to the world, to his world, just as they bind his interiority so that uncontrollable derelictions and nostalgia are neutralized. There where she was, we find, in the present, a 'there is' in which the other takes place with a status equal to any being-there. Leaving such a universe in order to meet the other in their difference is necessary if we want to begin remembering her. As is necessary the discovery of a self-affection in which she has not blindly shared. The masculine subject has to discover a

Being of his own that is not merely an unrecognized Being-to-the-other. Such a self-affection arranges a place for the 'here' in which the subject can hold himself within himself and return to himself, which permits him to let the other be. And to let the other be there, a 'there' that is no longer situated in my own world – that does not depend on me just as I do not depend on it. A 'there' that is outside of my 'here', just as the 'here' of the other takes place in a world that is foreign to me and of which I am, in this sense, the irreducible 'there'.

In fact, the other is there and not there with respect to me. To be sure, the other appears to me in a place of my space that is a 'there' in relation to my 'here', but the 'here' that animates the other does not amount to my 'there'. Apparently there, the other is also elsewhere, there where I cannot apprehend him, or her. And if in a work carried out together, something of this other can be revealed to me, it is nevertheless only an aspect of their Being, an aspect that already corresponds, at least in part, to an alienation of their freedom. Because the other is not reducible to what is common and because through their work the other is already put into the past. It is in my relation with him, or her, as other – and not as a same belonging to a common world – that the other can exist. I then return the other to the care for his, or her, freedom, a freedom that always entails a certain dereliction, or a certain terror, but is the condition for an authentic meeting between two subjects. A real assistance, and even foresight, towards the other demands just as much, if not more, a withdrawal before him, or her, in order to leave them to their space, as it does an intervention, indeed a breaking, into this space in order to lend them assistance. Rather than inviting the other to share the same world, the question is of releasing them from the world – mine, but also his or hers – in order to return them to a freedom that lies before any confinement in a network of relations that imprison them in an inextricable fate.

The world into which I enter already consists of an intertwining of meanings which will prevent me from discovering and communicating a sense that would be proper to me. The world into which I enter may protect me from the terror experienced in the face of a vast freedom and solitude, but it constitutes a prison that separates me from myself, from the other, and from the world each one could discover for oneself and the world that we could build together. A 'together' which would no longer correspond to participating in a common world that is already there and imposed on the two. A 'together' which implies that each one has to discover and assume a world of one's own, and that each one deliberately agrees to venture beyond one's world to open up to the world of the other and build, in respect for difference, for differences, a shared world. A world not always already given and imposed but elaborated by the two without belonging to either of the two. A world always future, transcendent to each one and in the construction of which the one and the other affirm their freedom while risking it – to the other. Without forgetting to come back to oneself for a gathering of one's self; which will preserve the energy devoted to work in common from becoming abstract, neutral, stereotyped or alienated by the other or the world built together.

For the philosopher, difference between us would be something secondary with respect to the undifferentiation of a collective 'one' to whom I belong as and with the others, the same as myself. Through my activity, I would try to merge into a common work, to equal, indeed surpass, others. I would thus attempt to distinguish myself without disowning my belonging to a collective 'one'. This 'one' – neutral, abstract, imperceptible and, nevertheless, more active upon reality than any singular subject – would impose on me, as on all others, its law. And every distinction between us could only take place inside the same and unique world already there.

This way of living presupposes that we are cut off, by the surrounding world, from the first relation with the one who gave birth to us, or, at least, who allowed us to enter into such an anonymous existence. It means to erase, to forget a particular relation with an other, a feminine other, who, on several accounts, is different from me and cannot be submitted to a gathering of equals to me. A difference, a real difference existed from my entry into the world, indeed before it. This first link, where substitution proves to be impossible, seems to be forgotten by the philosopher when it represents one of the first – ontic and ontological – reasons for the impossibility of substituting for the other. It also represents one of the paradigms of dependence, a dependence that is not a dependence on a 'one' already there but on an other irreducible to anyone. It is a question of an original dependence on a real and particular person. The mother is not a 'one', except for someone who wants to neutralize her. The mother is a precise 'who', a 'who' irreducible to another, who has helped me to enter into existence, to come into the world, without for all that relieving me of my task with regard to my existence. This first relation, essential for the constitution of subjectivity, seems to have escaped the attention of the phenomenologist. He forgets that the first surrounding world is not the public world of the 'one'. This world perhaps corresponds to the 'one' that I formed with my mother without yet being able to form a 'we' with her.

It is to this first 'one', this first undifferentiated community with the mother, that I must return in order to regain a unity in my subjectivity, still to be discovered and cultivated. If I do not return to this first world where I began to exist, I cannot have access to my real being. The 'one' of daily public existence already hides this first dual 'one' that I formed with my mother. From this 'one' I have to differentiate a 'you' and an 'I' in order to go from the undifferentiated 'one' to a 'we' formed by two singular selves respectful of their difference(s).

According to the philosopher, there is an abyss between the public 'one' in which my being-there would originate and the discovery of my authentic self. This abyss can be explained, at least in part, by the oblivion of the primitive dual relation with the mother and the necessity of a passage from this undifferentiated relation to a daily differentiated being two. When an 'I' and a 'you' are able to enter into presence with respect for their difference(s), they can emerge from the public 'one' in order to discover their proper self. A self who is now a more real, concrete and everyday self than the public 'one', because it does not evade the first 'one' in which it constituted itself, and henceforth it takes into consideration the relation to the other as an original dimension of its being in the world. Then it is not a question of an other already broken up and scattered in a collective 'one' which feeds on this other while forgetting it – hence its character, elusive and abstract from the real, whatever its impact on the reality of everyday life – but of this quite real and concrete other, the first 'who' with whom we are in relation: our mother.

No doubt she is elusive also, and for reasons of dependence as well, an elusiveness and dependence that are different from those of the 'one', but of which there are some traces remaining in the relation we live with respect to the 'one'. These two links envelop us, the two precede our entry into the world and continue after it. The two impose their law on us whether we do not consider them to be what they are. The one and the other are both within us and outside us. We can situate them with respect to us and apprehend their objectivity only with difficulty. Nevertheless, they are there, with a presence more insistent than any being encountered within the world in which we are, even if we cannot approach them, even if they never enter into presence but are present in that which allows the entry into presence of all.

Except the other as such. As long as the mother has not been recognized as the first other, and the 'one' as a sort of substitution for the relation with the mother, the other is merged in these never present presences, from which it cannot emerge. An unresolved link with the mother, an originary lack of recognition of her existence, irreducible to our own, leave us submerged in an undifferentiated collective 'one' in which each is confused with the other but without a possible meeting between us – merged together, we are also separated by a fundamental ignorance in the relation with the other.

Sharing in the Maternal World

Only a return to a something still more original, to the woman in the mother, to an identity different from ours, without any link of past dependence on it, allows us to prepare the space and the time in which it will be possible for us to enter into the presence of the other, with the other. The transcendence of this other, irreducible to us, can free the space of every weaving that is already there, at least for the time of a suspense – one that grants us the perception of what the difference is in its transcendental character. Later, we forget it and go back to our world. This experience of suspension and opening of our horizon will often have to be repeated in order that, little by little, we familiarize ourselves with the existence of an altogether other who apparently coexists with us in the same world. Such a gesture marks the passage to another space-time in the one to which we have grown accustomed. It arranges the possibility of another time in the one in which we live. It introduces us to a beyond in regard to our here and now.

To be sure, if the relationship of connivance and relational weaving is established between a solitary subject and its universe of objects, the opening to the other will be difficult. It is necessary to again pass through the first link with the mother as a relation to a 'who' never really recognized as such. This recognition of the mother as a 'who' can lead to the comprehension that her world is constituted in a different way from the world of the child with whom she is pregnant, whom she breast-feeds, whom she helps to enter into the world. The 'who' of the mother and the 'who' of the child do not inhabit the same world: the environment that they create through their doing or their being is not the same, and it is not possible to make them coexist as equal in a common world. The two are in the world, but the world in which they dwell is not the same. The world is real, concrete for each one, nevertheless it is not the same. There is a sharing of worlds in a sense, but of different worlds where each has different cares towards the other. The 'between' that links together the mother and the child, the child and the mother, does not amount to a subject–object relation. Masculine theories and practices have tried to convince us that this was the case. But if it was really so, the mother could not give assistance to the life of the child, and there would not be a space for coexistence between them.

Now this space exists and it exists between two 'who(s)', although they share it in different ways. To speak like the philosopher, each of these two 'who(s)' constitutes for each one a 'there' in which the other has a part. These two 'theres' are irreducible to a common world in which 'someone(s)' coexist. Each one experiences a unity in the relation with the other but these two 'one(s)' are neither equal nor can they substitute for one another, nor do they complement each other or compose as two a 'one' that would amount to those 'one(s)' of whom Heidegger speaks.

The relation that unites the mother and the child is authentic even if it is not accomplished as human. And to talk of a perfection of love with regard to the mother–child relation seems to me to be a mistake – it is not yet a relation between two human beings who freely assume to enter into relation with one another and to construct such a relation in time. Moreover, the participation of the whole being in the relation is not possible, as it can be between lovers. Certainly a totality is at stake for the child as well as for the mother, and even a reciprocity. But this totality and reciprocity do not amount to those of which two adults are capable who are autonomous with respect to one another and who take on their particularity and their difference(s), thus two adults who are not two 'one(s)'.

What will become of this world shared between two 'who(s)' in the common public world made up of many equal 'one(s)' who can a priori be substituted for one another? What has been forgotten by the philosopher? What have we forgotten such that we come to be reduced to anonymous individuals on whom a common world is a priori imposed? A world in which what links the components together and settles the patterns of organization is defined before we enter into it. Thus, without us. All that would be left to do is to submit to it, becoming machine-tools at its service. Each 'one' then represents a small unity of work comparable with another, with others – with varying degrees of performance between them.

What have we forgotten that makes us experience some particular mood in a given situation without being capable of understanding the origin of this mood? So much so that we want to approach the world, indeed the other, in a neutral and objective manner rather than with our whole being, including our sensitivity, our feelings, our imagination. Into what have these been invested, harnessed? Where are they held captive, reappearing only symptomatically without us being able to master their origin or their becoming? Where does what we perceive of ourselves in some context or other, in the manner of an affect blind with regard to our understanding, which we try to evade, come from? Have we not forgotten to establish passages and bridges between our past world and the world in which we are now situated? Could the dereliction we experience before the world in which we are be explained, at least in part, by the fact that we forget to situate in it she who has been the company and the mediator of our first being in the world? Why intend, henceforth, to assume all by ourselves the burden of existence in the world without concerning ourselves about the help that has been given to us in order to enter into this world?

No doubt the assistance cannot remain what it was for a child, but at least it can revive the memory that we do not live alone in the world nor only by ourselves. Before being solitary subjects in charge of some decision or other, we are and remain beings in relation. Such a truth changes what can be discovered concerning our being in the world as well as the manner of experiencing it. Neither mood nor dereliction nor other feelings appear as being of the same nature and they cannot be explained in the same way if we consider them from a relational point of view irreducible to the artificial facticity of a 'one'.

Taking care of one's own existence presupposes taking into account this interrelational dimension that constitutes an essential part of the human existence, and ensures it a very particular sort of subsistence. This seems to have been forgotten by the philosopher. The weaving of being in the world by multiple intersubjective relations – beginning with those with the mother – seems to have escaped his analyses of our existence. Hence the way of being affected by the world is both too immediate and too abstractly distanced by the anonymity of the 'one' and its web of utilitarian networks. A transition, a mediation between a merely bodily affect – for example, to be burnt by fire, to get wet with water, etc. – and a more global affection is lacking. The affect is too immediate because the passage through self-affection is missing; it is also too abstract because it lacks the dimension of transference of the first affects felt in the relation with the mother. They exist of course, but they are neutralized in a world presumed to be always already there, a world resulting from the work of 'one(s)', more or less competent but fundamentally equal and who can be substituted for one another. In such an affection by the world, the specifically human dimension is forgotten: the dimension of the relation to oneself, and of the relation to the other.

According to the philosopher, what affects us would only be that which, in the world in which we are situated, resists what is self-evident: that which resists us, that which cannot be of use to us, that which interrupts the familiarity of a world always already there. That which impedes our habits, or troubles our usual way of being in the world. But this way of being could amount to no more than a mere utilitarian apprenticeship in a knowing how to manage in life, to which are added affects resulting from a previous relation to the world whose transference in the present life is misjudged. In that earlier relation to the world, the relation with the mother and her mediation were decisive. But the philosopher does not take them into account when elaborating his phenomenology. And if he recognizes that some affects arise in the relation to the world, he does not allude to the possibility that they might come from a previous relational world which colours the way of experiencing the present situation. Instead he tries to erase this dimension of being in the world through processes of substitution, notably a substitution for the project of the other.

Concern, in fact, can be interpreted as a way of substituting oneself for the mother, which a process of reversal makes difficult to decipher. The subject, the 'one', concerns itself with that which surrounds it just as the mother was concerned with it. Often it will be to objects that one will repay the attention that the mother has paid to it: it is another difference that makes the process of substitution difficult to uncover. The third important change: the care of the 'one' for the objects or things of the world is determined by one's own need for survival. And one further point: if, in its concern, the 'one' being in the world substitutes itself for the mother, the world also substitutes itself for the mother. The mother was concerned with providing for the needs of the child, and the subject is concerned with providing for its needs thanks to the world. Its project with respect to the objects of the world or the world in general is the manner through which it escapes, or tries to escape, this first relational situation. In this way the philosopher gives to his subject a margin of freedom; at least, he attempts to do so. Such a project usually assumes its impetus from an energy awakened in the relation with the mother, a relation in which need to a great extent determined the moving-towards. The project is another way of again making one's own the impulse towards the other, but it transforms, in a predetermined gesture and a confinement within a given horizon, what can only be freed by recognizing the part of the other in the move-towards. Returning to this earlier situation is necessary so that a project can correspond to a freedom that remains a faithfulness to oneself and one's own possibilities.

Moreover, to be a real freedom, the project also must take into account the other met here and now. The return to the first relational world happens through an unveiling, not of the other as such, but of the existence of a relation that acts upon our way of perceiving and inhabiting the world. The latter is not determined only by history in general – a sort of construction carried out by countless 'one(s)' belonging to different epochs – but is also influenced by the story that I have lived since my coming into the world. No doubt, the relation with the mother is likely to become a generalizable element in the interpretation of humanity as such and of its history, but it also remains an irreducible particular component of each existence.

This does not mean that the mother as such already corresponds to the irreducible otherness of the other with whom I meet in adulthood. Such an aspect exists, but because the relation is not yet intersubjective, in the sense of being between two subjects autonomous with regard to one another, the irreducibility of the other as other is difficult to establish. What has to be recognized is the fact that the mother had a part in the world of the child as another subject situated at a different level from that of the child. The mother is, and remains, a 'You' rather than a 'you'. Her transcendence with respect to the world of the child is vertical rather than horizontal. And to this vertical transcendence has to be added the sexuate belonging of the mother, and of its relation to that of the child. In order to elaborate a relational project, the subject must rediscover the dimensions of the original relation with the mother that act upon his, or her, own world. Having reduced the mother to a natural pole in the formation and becoming of subjectivity, our tradition has been prevented from wondering about the importance of the relation to the other as such in human existence.

Language as Placental Dwelling/Language as Dialogue in Difference

All the more so in that discourse has been constituted with the aim of organizing the world into a significant whole at the disposal of the subject. The world would then double what exists through a gathering that makes it available, in particular by designating, naming and setting into a whole all that exists. Discourse, in some way, amounts to a double of the real that makes it handy for each one who comes into the world. Discourse becomes the world in which the subject dwells, a world that both ties the subject to and separates the subject from the existing real. This doubling of the existing real in which the subject dwells substitutes itself for the mother who was the first home. Discourse substitutes itself for the original world in which life has begun, which prevents us both from remembering it and from communicating with it – with her. Unless one wonders about the world, and in particular the discursive world, that constitutes one's present dwelling – a world which would correspond to one's Being.

This fabricated house, which is supposedly safeguarding Being, as much prevents Being. It prevents communication with this first other who is the mother, and makes exchanges with any other dependent on an artificial construction of the world.

Of course, language ensures a certain permanence of existence. But, since it is based on codes that immortalize only one moment of it, this language does not allow a faithfulness to life, to growth, to an encounter with the other. It fixes an appearing there where it ought to assist becoming while ensuring subsistence.

Our language, above all, constitutes a whole. If the philosopher considers that this whole comes from the world that he expresses, it is also possible to say that it is determined by the need for unity that the subject experiences. Language taken as a whole would be the relay of the totality that the child lived in the relation with the mother – whether this totality is imagined as one's own or as that of the mother. Language would exist as a substitute for the mother, or rather as a substitute for the relation with the mother. Hence, the fact of comparing it to a shelter, a house. If this really is the case, language intervenes between the subject and the world as an unthought effect of a relation with the first other who has allowed us to come into the world, to enter the world.

We cannot listen to this first other starting from a single and shared whole. In a certain sense, we cannot listen to this other as such. What it – or rather she – says does not belong to a common world in which we already are: a world already understood, clarified, used by us. What she says makes a common world exist, a world that is relational before being utilitarian. In other words: in our initial world, the relational dimension includes the utilitarian dimension, at that time corresponding to vital needs. In the world of the child, being with the other includes and determines being with objects or things. And to transform the mother into a thing – as Freud did in interpreting little Hans's game with the bobbin – does not resolve the question of the first perception of the world by the child. Such a gesture begins to substitute for the first one another world, a world that intends to do without it through mastering it. But, in fact, the first world remains below the world made up by the child, of which it will in part determine the horizon, the affects, the links between things and the subject, as well as between things themselves.

It is the mother who first brings us into the world. The world she gives to us, and to which she gives us, is necessarily present in our way of experiencing the world and of living in the world. But the philosopher has not yet considered this. He pays no attention and even forgets this original determination of our way of being in the world. He thus cannot take into account the in-finite involved in the relation with the mother. And his apprehension of the world requires an a priori reversal: the relation with the other will be included in the relation with the world, and not the contrary. From then on, subjectivity will be deprived of an origin and singularity – it will correspond to a 'whoever', a some 'one' or 'anybody' defined by a world that existed before it. The priority given to an idea of the world – even a concrete world – with respect to the relation with the other, the first other, exiles subjectivity from its being in a real world. It enters an anonymous, impersonal, indefinite world: a world of 'one(s)', or 'there is'. The relation with the other is imposed by a common belonging to a world that is already there. To enter into relation with the other obeys the necessity of participating in a common world, indeed in a shared mood towards this world.

Whatever he says, the philosopher then remains in an informational discourse. The words through which a particular subject addresses another particular subject in order to communicate something about oneself, taking into account the other as other, do not exist, and their use remains groundless. There are no words going from the interiority of the one to the interiority of the other, Heidegger wrote. Does this not mean: going from the Being of the one to the Being of the other? And is not the forgetting of Being, among other things, the result of this ignorance of the Being whom we are? A Being for whom the relation with the other, and with ourselves, is not simply ordered by the impact of a supposedly objective world on our subjectivity, in particular in its intersubjective dimension.

According to Heidegger, being in the world would always amount to being outside oneself, which can be understood in various ways. In Heidegger's opinion, the relations with the other cannot take place at the level of interiority because it is starting from an outside of each one that we enter into communication. But is this not to forget that the other, in particular the first other, has become ourselves? That this first other takes place within us and not only outside of us, and that a more or less well-accomplished internalization determines our manner of apprehending the world? This is so because the first other has been assimilated with the air that we have breathed, the milk that we have drunk, the words that we have heard, words which at first amounted to the tone of a voice rather than to the sharing of a discourse. The other has thus become us without our knowing it and is present in us when we now perceive the world. This world is not a mere facticity. It is already inhabited by a presence, most of the time not recognized, that gives it a certain horizon and is the source of certain affects. Failing to take care of this, we place ourselves in relation to the world just as a child does in relation to its parents, in particular to the mother: we receive and obey the world in some way, we assent to it or we refuse and reject it, we rebel against it in the manner of a challenge or an aversion. We have not yet reached the stage of a reciprocal listening, with some questioning, the stage of a creation of meaning resulting from the relation, and an interaction linked to a present meeting and not from the always already planned. Our discourse is generally determined by a world that already exists: it does not arise from the relation with the other as such. Hence our conviction that the other is the bearer of a speech which is dependent on the already existing world and not a speech of their own, disclosing to us a world different from the world in which we dwell. Which is the only way of giving us back to ourselves, of freeing us from the ascendancy of an environing world that is already there, a world we inhabit and share only from force of habit and under duress, without having made it ours through perception or creation.

In this environment the projection of an unrecognized relation with the mother mingles with what we have learned through our coming into a world that is already there. This environment is not our own, but it conceals from us the real that we would like to approach. It especially veils from us the other – whose otherness is imperceptible to us as long as the relation with the mother is not recognized and the world in which we dwell substitutes itself for this relation, as it has for centuries. This has led us to confuse the other with an object of the world, an other from whom we are separated both by the relation with a first other and by its reduction to an object.

The other then remains imperceptible, not because of otherness, but because of that which conceals otherness. I may imagine being able to discover the other as a reality of my world and through a sharing of this world. From such a perspective, I bend the other to my horizon and he, or she, loses their own existence, unless they escape my apprehension and disappear from my world. The other invites me to a conversion in the way of perceiving the real. In fact, the other never appears in his, or her, otherness: what makes them other is never revealed, except partially, in a roundabout way and by induction. The other as other escapes my gaze.

A logic that favours sight precludes coexistence and communication with the other as other. All the assessments of difference in the relation to the other will then become only quantitative, that is to say, appraised according to the same scale. And we consider the other as being more or less worthy in comparison to us but not as different, and living in a world in which other values exist.

We do not see the other as such, just as we have not seen our mother, the first other with whom we have been in relation, even if the motive is not the same in both cases. The other is still and always to be discovered. And what people or collective opinion say about this other cannot, in their facticity and chattering, unveil who he, or she, is. And what the other has already tried to express of himself, or herself, does not necessarily correspond to who they are. Because, who has already been to the source of one's Being, and succeeded in saying something about it to the other? Only a few sages have ventured down the path to the heart of themselves, most often in solitude and by making use of an Absolute, supposedly foreign to them, in order to accomplish their journey. They have not merely withdrawn from their links with the world, with others, with their past, in order to inquire about what or who they were beyond all such belonging or co-belonging. They created another company in order to support, to identify, to reflect themselves. And often they attributed to some Other – God, Ideal, Idea – what they had discovered about themselves.

Wondering about oneself, about what or who we are after having renounced the environment that has consti-tuted and bound us, seems to make us too dizzy to venture upon such a task. And since man has never met with himself, it is thus difficult for us to meet with him, except by giving up apprehending anything of him. Or by agreeing to become an assistance to the unveiling of their Being by the other – remaining a pure presence that is held in itself, without overflowing the limits of oneself or being reduced for all that to nothing or to some a priori. Pure breath? Of which the reserve – the soul? – allows us to pay attention to the other in a suspension of our own becoming. Because if such a task were to be the only one to which one devotes oneself, one would soon stop being. Holding one's breath in order to listen to the other without a project or an a priori, other than to help the other to be, exceeds our possibilities as living beings if such a gesture intends to be permanent and univocal. In the meeting with the other, it belongs to each one to keep on hold one's own becoming in order to lend assistance to the other's becoming. Not by concerning oneself with only some aspect of their present existence, but by making oneself a presence assisting the other in turning back to themselves, in the discovery of what or who they are and their faithfulness to this disclosure.

We have not yet reached such a coexistence with the other, or we have already forgotten it. A logic that favours the object, and a perception from a distance that allows a grasping of this object, prevents an economy of inter-subjectivity from being revealed to us. Here touch would be the necessary medium – as light and silence are for seeing and listening. But then touch is no longer the mere immediacy of which the philosopher talks, an immediacy that metaphysics has appropriated in its logic of representation. Touch becomes the medium par excellence of interiority. The relation between touching and being touched is displaced within the subject, where it articulates a relation between active and passive that requires the passage to another space-time. For the subject to experience himself, or herself, as both affecting and affected, an inward space must be created in which the two take place thanks to a temporal delay in which the active relates to the passive. Such an operation can be expressed by the middle-passive voice.

We do not know, or we no longer know, this space-time of the middle-passive voice. Returning to and cultivating it is necessary in order to be able to enter into relation with the other as other. If I have not constituted in myself and for myself the process of self-affection, then, in the relations with the other, affect often becomes the abolition of the one or of the other. There will no longer be two subjects relating to one another without the mediation of a third drawing both of them away from a nearness to self, thus virtually away from a nearness to the other. Metaphysics seems to have been elaborated in order to allow us to escape an immediate nearness with another living being. It has not arrived at the point of constituting a dialectics of the relations with the other(s) in which touch itself would be the mediation. However, it is this mediation that we need in order to establish such a relational economy. Self-affection creates an autonomous space-time for the child with respect to the mother. And it is through self-affection – as it provides an inward autonomous space-time – that nearness with the other becomes possible in remoteness. But such nearness and remoteness differ from those envisioned by the Western philosopher. Respecting my own self-affection in the relation to the other, I create a space-time that finds a horizon and becomes a world if I also respect the self-affection of the other. Solely inward space provides itself with an outward space, thanks to which the encounter and coexistence with the other become possible.

Such an inward – and also outward – space is not lighted up like the world generally perceived outside of ourselves: it participates in another light. As with the sun and yet otherwise, the light that acts as mediation in perception is not perceptible as such, at least not completely and in a thematic manner. It acts on us without becoming an object of apperception. It is thus present in the perception of objects and the constitution of the world but, in a way, imperceptibly.

The same applies to the other who enlightens us, notably through desire: the desire that we experience as ours as well as that of the other. Such light enters into us but we do not distinguish its source. And we often confuse our desire and that of the other by thinking that, as is the case for the sun, it is a question of a unique source of energy, of light. We thus abolish the limits between the other and ourselves. We artificially become one, which leads to the loss of the one, the other and the desire between us. We then merge into and with the masses, imagining that we are all animated by the same desire. Which can be true with respect to a common third but not to desire for the other as other.

Afterword

The other as such has been excluded from the elaboration of Western culture. The main aim of this culture has been to allow man to differentiate himself from his maternal origin, an origin confused with the natural world. Man has tried to affirm himself by dominating his natural belonging and the environing world related to it, notably through a partnership, but also through a competition, with those who are like him. The other as other did not share in this society and culture between men, except, for example, as an elder able to provide guidance or a youth needing guidance. Indeed difference was assessed in a quantitative and not a qualitative way, in particular with regard to the aptitude for bringing under control the living and sensible world and transforming it into a constructed world appropriate to man.

Henceforth, we perceive the limits of this culture, whether this be on the side of truth and ethics or on the side of the danger that it represents for human life and consciousness. The specific character of this culture is also revealed through the discovery of other civilizations, which are far from appearing barbarous compared to ours.

The current multicultural era opens us up to perspectives on the relative aspects of our tradition. We believed our world to be the only one, but we discover that it is a partial and incomplete evolution of humanity. A part, until now unrecognized, of our truth can be revealed to us thanks to the other, if we accept to partially open our own horizon in order to perceive and welcome the other as other without intending to dominate, to colonize, or to integrate this other into our past.

To recognize the share of truth that the other conveys can help us to resolve certain challenges of our time.

Discovering the limited and sometimes erroneous character of our cultural construction can lead us to a destructive nihilism with respect to all our values, including that partial individualization which man has, with difficulty, gained. No doubt, to pass from one epoch to another requires an interpretative and critical attitude towards the past, but not necessarily a total destruction of our tradition. The other, insofar as this other takes place on this side of or beyond our world, can open up a path towards an elaboration of another cultural era, because this other exists outside of our own horizon and because their values and logic are not the same as those of our tradition. It is because the other belongs to another world, and insofar as they remain faithful to it, that the other offers us a chance for a future. One could also say: a means of overcoming nihilism without forgetting its teaching. In order to meet the other, to exchange with the one who dwells in a world different from ours, we must return to our overall identity and not confine ourselves to a cultural construction which claims to surmount our living and sensible being. The other also compels us to take upon ourselves the negative – that is to say, to provide ourselves with limits in order to let the other be as other. The other opens us to the possibility of another era for our subjective becoming and for our culture. The other introduces us to another logic in which the relational values, notably of coexistence in difference, are considered and cultivated and not only the values of mastery and know-how and their extension-expansion, which are necessarily accompanied by warlike and conflictual competitions between those who are alike. And let us recall that in our tradition, the other is at first woman, beginning with woman in the mother.

Learning to coexist with the other, the one left outside the construction of our tradition, initiates us into a global coexistence that corresponds to one of the challenges of our epoch. To open a place for the other, for a world different from ours, from the inside of our tradition, is the first and the most difficult multicultural gesture. Meeting the stranger outside of our own boundaries is rather easy, and even satisfies our aspirations, as long as we can return home and appropriate between ourselves what we have in this way discovered. To be forced to limit and change our home, or our way of being at home, is much more difficult, especially without being unfaithful to ourselves. This requires us to elaborate a different subjectivity from that which has for centuries been ours, a subjectivity for which coexistence and exchange only took place between those who were alike and inside a single tradition. Nature then remained, moreover, a part of an uncultivated familiarity that was preserved inside the walls of the private dwelling place. A nature that man continued endeavouring to dominate and make his own, especially through his wife and children. A nature that was not respected as such, but subjected to male instincts and passions. A nature that man persists in wanting to control, and despise, beyond the wife and the child, in the other race, the other ethnic community and all that reminds him of a natural belonging. As long as the other is not recognized and respected as a bridge between nature and culture, a bridge that gender at first is, every attempt to establish a democratic globalization will remain a moral imperative without concrete fulfilment. As long as the universal is not considered as being two, and humanity as being a place of fruitful cultural coexistence between two irreducibly different genders, a culture will never stop imposing its colour and values upon another, including through its morality and religion.

This requirement results both from a failure to cultivate our own instincts and from a need for transcendence which ends in wanting to impose our transcendence – our God, our Truth, our Good – on others in order to safeguard it as our own. In such a will, a natural immediacy continues to be exerted under the cover of an absolute ideal. We know the ravages that this relation to transcendence is capable of causing towards persons or between various traditions. The means of remedying this would be to educate about transcendence in the relation to an other irreducible to oneself, beginning with the other of sexuate difference. Respect for the other as standing beyond the limits of one's own world – that is, for the other as transcendent to me and to my horizon – disciplines the immediacy of the need to go beyond our limits. This need, originally natural and vital, can develop as an instinct for possession, for appropriation or domination to the detriment of the other, or it can be cultivated as a specifically human way to enter into relation with the different other, whose irreducibility is recognized. Taking into consideration this horizontal and qualitative transcendence trains our sensibility, provides limits that permit it to be cultivated and attain a transcendental character. If we search in a vertical transcendence for an absolute perfection with regard to ourselves, respect for the horizontal transcendence of the other allows us to aim at this perfection without for all that intending to impose it as the only one possible.

Cultivating our sensibility, including our corporeal sensibility, in order to enter into relation with a different other is also a way to escape the nihilism threatening our tradition as well as its critique. To decide in favour of the human truth that we can be and want to be in relation to and with the other amounts to being faithful to a different truth from the one, dependent on a supra-sensible absolute, that has both exiled us from ourselves and separated us from one another.

The existence of the total and always already differentiated real that we are can be approached, affirmed, and expressed to the other through art. Not only through the work of art that we create outside of ourselves, but the one that we can become by transforming, at each moment, our natural immediacy into a way of being likely to exchange with the other. To be both the artist and the work of art is our task in relating with the other, beginning with the other who is sexually different from us. This requires a safeguarding and a cultivation of our affects, notably through the constitution and preservation of a self-affection of our own.

Self-affection is the real dwelling to which we must always return with a view to a faithfulness to ourselves and an ability to welcome the other as different. Self-affection corresponds to an art of interiority, of internalization, that we have to discover, to invent, to cultivate, and to express: in ourselves and between us. Such an art can lead the way towards our becoming universal and convivial beings, capable of coexistence with all differences. This art is thus the mediation necessary for constructing together a shareable world.

We cannot share the world as it already is, with the exception of the natural world. The world in which we might coexist in mutual respect cannot be founded on solely supra-sensible values nor on a division between natural and cultural belonging. Nor can it be based on necessities corresponding to merely a part of humanity that has existed in a certain place on the earth and at a certain epoch of human evolution. The world that we can share is always and still to be elaborated by us and between us starting from the perception and affirmation of what and who we are as humans here and now. Humans who endeavour to use their own energy as well as that arising from their difference in order to create: to create themselves, to help the other to create himself or herself while accepting their help, and to create a world in which we can live in peace and happiness while working towards the becoming of humanity starting from the natural belonging and world that are our own.